I CAN AND I WILL

I CAN AND I WILL

AUTOBIOGRAPHY OF YASH GUPTA MBE

Text Yash Gupta and Radhika Kapur

Design Grade Design, London

Copyright © Yash Gupta & Story Terrace

Text is private and confidential

First print March 2016

www.StoryTerrace.com

CONTENTS

ACKNOWLEDGEMENTS

I would like to thank my children and grandchildren for their encouragement to write this autobiography, which I hope will inspire young people to fulfil their dreams. As a first generation immigrant I had to struggle hard to keep my dream alive against all the hurdles of colour prejudice, no cash, and a number of rejections for getting my first suitable job. However, I never lost my determination, and followed the motto – "I can and I will".

I would like to thank Story Terrace for their help, and a special thank you to Radhika Kapur for editing the book and Emily McCracken for getting it printed. Yash

1. A TERRIBLE SEPARATION

The raging river Ravi had burst free of its banks and dead bodies floated past us. However, the crushing fear that we might be attacked by a Muslim mob led us and the other escaping villagers of *Kanjrur Dattan,* the town in Pakistan in which I was born and had lived all my life, to jump into it in our desperate attempt to reach free India.

My father gripped my sweaty hand tight as he and my mother carried my three siblings on their backs and started to walk into the turbulent waters, stoically. God knows if we would have survived if not for the army soldiers that appeared in their boat.

Holding onto the sides of the boat with frantic fingers, we clambered on along with a few other families. Thankfully, we reached the other side safe, but I witnessed a large number of my town folk including women, children and elders being washed away in the swollen river. They paid a heavy price for the freedom of India.

The 15th of August, 1947 – it was on this fateful day that Free India was declared. Pakistan came into existence a day earlier. The British packed their suitcases and left behind a country in utter turmoil. What followed was a bloodcurdling nightmare – the killing, looting and burning of both Hindus and Muslims on either side of the border.

I yearned for the idyllic days of my childhood when everyone in the town – Hindus, Muslims, Sikhs, Christians and upper and lower caste – played together. This was despite the advice of the priest from the nearby Hindu temple, who told us not to interact with the lower caste folk, but whom I happily ignored. My mother and grandmother let us play with everyone, but being orthodox Hindus asked us to share food with only those from the top three Hindu Castes: Brahmins, Khatris and Baniyas.

Kanjur Dattan was a small place where everyone knew everyone. Both my father and grandfather were born there. The older people were addressed as grandparents, adults were called uncles and aunties and older children were brothers and sisters. I come from a big family of four brothers and four sisters. The only one I did not have the pleasure of playing with in my early childhood was my elder brother as he had been living with my maternal grandparents from the age of three. He was nearly two and a half years older than me. I was finally reunited with him at the age of twelve when we migrated from Pakistan to new India. I will talk about him in detail in the next chapter. My other siblings there were Swaran, Raj and Surinder. The rest were born in India.

I was five years old when I started my education at the local primary school. My father held my small palm in one hand and a box of sweet laddoos in the other as we walked the long half-mile from our house to the school building. The closer it got, the tighter I held onto his hand. I was both excited and nervous, he later told me. He handed me over to the teacher and gave him the box of sweets and so started my very first day at the school, where I was to spend the next six years of my life.

I quickly recognised two boys from my street and sat next to them on the floor. There were about 60 or 70 of us. The teacher appeared to be very strict and kept waving his stick about to keep us quiet. All through primary school that stick scared the life out of me, although it was always the same two or three boys who would bear the brunt of it each time. There were usually two monitors in the class – strong, tall and well-behaved boys who would help to maintain discipline in the classroom. Sadly, as I was a boy of small stature I never got the chance to be one.

Most of the teachers at school came from the Muslim community and we called them Maulvi Sahib. The language of instruction was Urdu. As you can see, life between the two communities was peaceful and integrated. We learnt reading, writing and numbers. There were a few lessons in History and Geography too. Every afternoon we would recite the tables from two to sixteen. I really enjoyed that and remember them still today.

In my childhood, I was greatly influenced by my mother. She looked after us very well in the absence of my father who spent most of his time in Amritsar, where he had a clerical job with a British Company called Rallies Brothers, which traded in cotton. Though my mother never went to school herself, she understood the importance of schooling for her children. I can still visualise her insisting that I tell her every thing that happened at school and sitting with me 'til I finished my homework. The way she used to direct my schoolwork, I could not believe it when she told me on my eighth birthday that she did not know how to read or write and could only count up to twenty! She was a great inspiration in all of our lives and provided counselling, support and care. All of her eight children, four sons and four daughters, adored her. I will go on mentioning her contribution to my life in the later chapters of this biography.

Being the eldest child in the house, I helped my mother in looking after my siblings when she had to sew other people's clothes to supplement the family income and fulfil our needs for clothes, books, toys and food. I would also write letters on her behalf to my dad when she wanted him to bring some things for the family urgently.

My mother, Shrimiti Lajwanti Devi, a tremendous influence in my life

My father would visit us five to six times a year. He'd come bearing new toys, clothes and sweets. My siblings and I would excitedly await his visits. Of course, we would behave very well in his presence, as he was a very strict parent.

Every year, I used to miss my school for nearly one month, as our family would spend time with him in Amritsar. The city is famous for the Golden Temple, a sacred place of worship for the Sikh community all over the world. I would go with my father to the Golden Temple once a week, and after taking a dip in the holy water we would go inside and pray for a few minutes. It was a wonderful religious experience. During these visits I developed a lot of affection and respect for my father, even though I always felt nervous in his presence and afraid to offend him with mischief.

There is one very significant event in my life that is associated with my visits to Amritsar. I was nearly six years old when my father took me to his office one day. If I remember correctly his job was to manually photocopy typed documents. At ten o'clock sharp there was a dead silence and I heard hushed voices whispering, "Sahib has arrived". My father quickly instructed me to hide behind a cupboard, but I was very curious to have a glimpse of this *Sahib* whose arrival had terrified everyone. Peeping through a small window I saw a glowing, hat-clad face. He was a middle-aged white man

My father, Shree Dina Nath

14

called Mr. Thomas. People said that he was the big boss and would talk to the head-clerk and no-one else. We left to get some food at lunchtime and my father pointed his car out to me. I saw Sahib's driver busy polishing it, making it gleam.

This incident left a huge impression on my tender mind and remained in my memory for many years to come. Perhaps it was this that motivated me to make a visit to Sahib's country – the UK, from where my country the big India had been ruled.

After finishing my primary school at the age of eleven, I started my secondary education in a Hindu school, D.A.V. High School, which was the only secondary school in our town. Most of my class fellows from the primary school joined and they all belonged to various religious communities. The school assembly started with Hindu prayers and most of the teachers were from the Hindu community, though there were a few Sikh and Muslim teachers as well. There was good communal harmony in my first year in the school.

Sinister shadows slowly started creeping in towards the end of first year and the start of second. The year was 1947 and the political tension in the country was rippling through the town as well as our school. There were some incidents of communal tension amongst the Muslim and Hindu students. Hindu and Sikh students shouted "Long live Mother India" and "Death to Pakistan"; Muslim students shouted "Death to India" and "Long live Pakistan" outside the boundary walls. Even the playground wasn't spared. Hindu and Sikh children stopped playing with Muslim students and vice versa. Ill-feeling penetrated the classroom despite the hard discipline enforced by our teachers.

By the May or June of 1947, discord had coalesced into hatred. The whole environment was pregnant with communal tension. We kept hearing news of riots breaking out in big cities all over India. My father came home as the riots spread as far as Amritsar.

A great mutual trust that had been built over centuries of living together was giving way to an atmosphere of fear, anger and anxiety. The school closed for the summer holidays. While the political leaders of both major parties – the Congress and the Muslim League – kept assuring people that we were safe and should stay put in our villages and towns, my father urged the town's people to do otherwise. His experiences in Amritsar had convinced him that the Hindus and Sikhs in Pakistan were not safe. He tried to persuade the town's elders to leave, but they neither believed him nor budged. They couldn't conceive the thought of leaving behind the only home they had ever known, that their forefathers had lived and died in, for some unknown, unmoored destination in a new India.

On the 14th of August 1947, Pakistan came into being and Free India the next day. It was supposed to be a joyous occasion, but in Punjab, rivers of blood flowed on both sides of the border. Law and order collapsed. However, there were still no incidents of killing and looting in our own town.

On the 1st of September 1947, a rumour spread in our area. Muslim Gangs from the neighbouring towns were going to attack the Hindu and Sikh households that night. The Hindu elders huddled and made a decision to leave town temporarily, only for a few days, until things settled down.

My parents locked our house and gave the keys to one of our Muslim friends who promised to look after it while we were away. Little did we know that we would never be back.

Nearly one thousand people, including my family, set off on foot, walking towards a nearby forest to take shelter. Heart-wrenchingly, some of the elders simply refused to leave. They said they would rather die than abandon their home – where generations of their family had been born and died.

Around midnight, some frightened people came running out from the direction of our town shouting, "Muslim gangs are looting our properties! They've killed the elders who stayed behind!" The mob knew that we were hiding in the forest, they said. They would soon come our way and turn their wrath on us. The elders decided that we must immediately start walking towards the Indian border, which was six miles away on the other side of the River Ravi.

All I can say is that it was the most horrific journey of my life. Silently moving lips and furiously beating hearts were praying for the safe crossing of the river, which in those days was as stormy and furious as the land through which it flowed. My parents had to carry my two young sisters Swaran and Raj and little brother Surinder in their arms for most of the way. My nine year-old sister and six-year-old brother walked for a few yards in the middle to give them some relief. Occasionally,

I would carry my sisters. The six miles to the border looked like a never-ending journey for most young children and their parents. And, when it was time to make the crossing, our eyes tremulously took in the Ravi in a gnashing, thrashing flood.

I have already described what happened when we and the other families gave our fates over to the waters and how we were saved by the army soldiers in their boats, unlike many of my town folk. I had never experienced the kind of fear that I did as those waters pulled at my ankles. To see loved ones perish in front of your own eyes is a fate I don't wish upon my worst enemies. We reached the border on the other side of the Ravi, traumatised and broken-hearted, and were taken to a refugee camp at Dera Baba Nanak. Young volunteers helped us with food and clothing. It slowly dawned on me that my family along with millions of other families had become the victims of a horrible religious cleansing, for no fault of their own. These innocent people, the unsung heroes, paid a truly heavy price for Independent India.

We who migrated to India after leaving our roots, ancestral property and wealth carried intense feelings of anger and hatred for the Congress Party and did not join in the celebrations of independence for many years to come. There were feelings of anger, disappointment and revenge amongst the people in the Refugee Camp. People were openly blaming the Gandhi-Nehru leadership for the tragedy. Perhaps it was these feelings of hatred that led to the tragic murder of Gandhiji in January 1948.

I myself harboured feelings of vengeance and bitterness towards the Congress leadership as well as the Muslim community for a long while. Some time later, we were rehabilitated in Dhariwal in Punjab. It was when we were given a house vacated by a Muslim family that it struck me that innocent, ordinary Muslims were also the victims of the same religious cleansing. My feelings towards ordinary Muslims softened, but not towards fanatics.

This experience of leaving my ancestral home, witnessing killings of blameless people and spending days in the refugee camp had a very deep emotional affect on me for almost all my life. This has impacted me in three ways:

1. My parents' financial difficulties forced me to start adult work at the tender age of twelve and also prevented me and my other siblings from continuing our education for a while.

2. My faith in the main political party, the Congress, and its leadership was totally shattered. My father and uncles told us again and again that the Congress Party under the leadership of Gandhi and Nehru had assured people that they would never ever accept Partition. Gandhi was even quoted saying that the partition of India would happen over his dead body. A funny laughter would bubble up in my throat when anyone reminded me of that. I felt that he did not die but a million innocent, ordinary people did. I never

trusted the Congress and always opposed their policies 'til the age of 31 when I left India for the UK.

3. During my days in the refugee camp, I was very impressed by the dedication of the volunteers who brought us food, clothing and medicines. I learnt that these young people giving their time and energy to help us belonged to the RSS or the Rashtryia Swayamsevak Sangh, a nationalist Hindu organisation (Although its membership is open to all Indians). When we settled in Dhariwal, I joined the local RSS branch at the age of twelve and remained influenced by its philosophy of selfless service for India and its ancient culture throughout my life.

2. A NEW BEGINNING

We stayed in the refugee camp in Dera Baba Nanak for nearly a month. Nearly a million innocent people had lost their lives in this religious cleansing and 14 million had been displaced. The camp was cramped, there was no electricity and the sanitary conditions were terrible, so it was difficult to adjust.

As law and order slowly limped back to normal, people scrambled to get in touch with relatives. I remember my father, writing letter after letter to my maternal grandparents who lived in the small village of Balore in Gurdaspur district in Punjab. He was finally able to make contact with my maternal uncle who lived with his family in Dhariwal, not too far from my grandparents. There was relief and tears as they too had been desperately trying to locate us. My uncle came to the refugee camp and we children rushed into his arms. He took us with him to his home in Dhariwal, where he worked in a British-owned woollen mill. We stayed with him for one month, in which he helped us secure a house that had been vacated by a Muslim family who had fled to the other side of the border.

The house was absolutely derelict, having been looted and vandalized by Hindu mobs. I often lay in bed wondering about the family that had lived here. What had happened to them? Had they survived the journey to Pakistan? My grandparents and uncles helped settle us in by providing us with basic goods and money so that we could live here safely.

My father had left his job in Amritsar, so he needed to start earning to keep the family going. My uncle gave him some money, with which he set up a small business of washing and dying clothes at the street corner. I did not resume my studies, but helped him so that the family could eat on a day-to-day basis. I learnt how to wash and dye clothes properly. My fingers slowly crinkled in the water and became stained with colour. It was all done manually in those days and since I was a lad of small stature, it was physically arduous for me.

After eight months, my father decided that I must continue my studies and sent me to my maternal grandparents. My elder brother, Satpal, whom I have mentioned in the earlier chapter, was also there. I found a peculiar situation there. There was no school in the village, so Satpal had only started going to a school – which was three miles away in the town of Dina Nagar – when he was seven years old. As a result, he and I were now in the very same class: Grade Seven!

Luckily, I didn't lose a year of my studies; the government had extended the academic year by three months because of the disturbances in the country. There were four other boys who were in the same school as us and we walked together every morning. I would feel quite fatigued, as I was not physically strong and only four feet tall and it was quite a distance to school. The other children would tease me a lot. "Midget!" they would call out and giggle furiously. However, the desire to study always blazed bright within me, so I worked hard to make up the lost months and thankfully passed the annual examination along with my elder brother.

I loved village life. It was so different compared to town life. Everyone cared for and supported one another. The children did not just belong to their own family, but to the whole village.

Life centred around the land – ploughing, sowing, watering and the looking after of crops until they were ripe for cutting. My grandfather also had agricultural land, two fruit gardens and a small grocery shop. We children would not go to school during the sowing and reaping seasons, but would help in the fields instead. In fact, the local school used to close at these times for holidays. After a hard day's work, everyone congregated in the centre of the village in the evening. There was a village radio and the men would gather around it and listen to Bollywood songs and the evening news. I can still hear the strains of *Aaj Meri Barbaad Mohabbat* wafting over the balmy evening breeze. The young people would wrestle and play Kabaddi and the children played their own games. Festivals like Baisakhi and Diwali were a time for collective celebration. My chappals would pound through dusty tracks as I ran to the local temple on festival days to collect the special sweets given out to the children after the prayers.

Life in the village existed in a soft cocoon. The outside world seemed far, far away. People had everything they needed for their day-to-day life – shops, moneylenders, physicians, barbers, shoemakers, carpenters, blacksmiths, cloth-makers, tailors and the priest. In fact, most local people hardly ever stepped out of the village. The cities might have been experiencing huge turmoil as regimes changed hands, but none of these changes touched village life and we continued to live blissfully.

My happy days were interrupted when my grandfather died of a heart attack at the age of 62. It was a great loss for us grandchildren and my grandmother.

My father decided to take my elder brother and me back to Dhariwal. While I was away, my sister Raksha had been born. Now that I think about it I do wonder why my parents went on having children even whilst struggling to feed us. Perhaps there were no birth control methods available to them and there was a tradition of having large families.

Back in Dhariwal, my elder brother and I continued our education at the DAV High School. The day would begin with prayers, exercises and was followed by the teaching of Hindi, Punjabi, Maths, History and Geography. I also chose to study Sanskrit as an optional subject. In the evenings, we would help our father in the shop and take up odd jobs to supplement the family income. Expenses were mounting as my younger brother and two sisters had also started school and my parents had to pay tuition fees for all of us except my brother and I. The Head Teacher had exempted me from the school fee for my academic achievements and my maternal uncle paid my elder brother's fees. In spite of all difficulties, my brother and I concentrated on our studies and we both passed our Matriculation examination from the Punjab University in March 1951, securing a First Class. I came second in a group of 120 students by securing 596 marks.

It was in those days that my sister Sudesh was also born. My elder brother decided to look for a job and he got part-

My Matriculation class, 1951

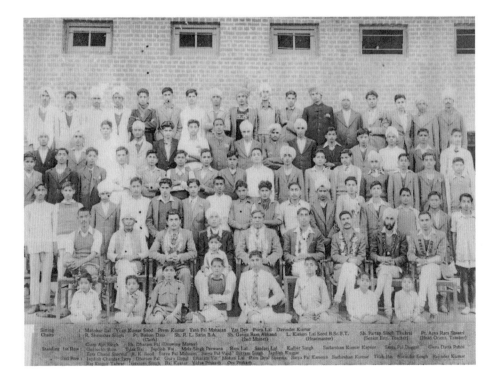

time work with a local shopkeeper whose business it was to prepare chapati flour for the local residents. He was just eighteen, but looked far more mature. I on the other hand was still only 4'10" and looked younger than my fifteen years. I was very keen to continue my education, but my parents could not afford to send me to the college, which was in a big town called Batala nearly twelve miles away. So, I became a pedlar and sold soap by going from village to village on foot. As it would exhaust me, I realised enough was enough and decided to focus on building my body. In six months I grew to 5'5" ! My face started looking more mature, much to my delight, and I got a job at the local woollen mill in October 1951 as a labourer and junior clerk – a memorable experience.

There were nearly twenty British men working at this British owned mill as heads of various departments. My job was in the packing department – a department of about 40 people. I was first employed to move the bales from one place to another and was later given the job of checking the addresses on the bales. Mr. Saunders, the head of this department, left the day-to-day administration to a local person. I hardly had any contact with Mr. Saunders. During my six months there, I was able to see the workings of all twelve departments. Big machines were used for washing the wool and manufacturing blankets, woollen clothes and many other items. It was a very educational experience, despite the fact that I had no intention of staying there all my life.

The uniqueness of Dhariwal was that this big woollen mill (one of two big woollen mills in the country owned by the British) brought a number of British people to our small town.

British influence was very visible there. They had an exclusive clubhouse, which was very much like a pub, a special shop filled with foreign goods just for them and a golf course. They built special homes and bungalows for themselves outside town, in an area forbidden to the locals. In fact, they hardly interacted with the natives. British architects must have built their houses, as they were very similar to the houses I saw in Slough when I settled there, after arriving in Britain. I now laugh when I remember their sliding roofs. What use were sliding roofs in a town with hardly any rainfall? Obviously the British carried their own architecture and culture with them when they came to India, just like any other immigrant community. They did not want to lose their roots.

They built a big church, a missionary high school, a missionary hospital and the Salvation Army headquarters in the town. As a result of conversions carried out by missionaries, nearly 15% of the population was Christian. Unlike other towns, Christmas was celebrated here with much gusto. There were a number of educated Christians in this town employed in the Mill and also in the school and other places. The Christian community here was very different to the one in my ancestral town in Pakistan. They had a higher status and were more educated unlike the community in my village, which was at the bottom of the social ladder and did menial jobs.

After independence, the woollen mill was bought over by an Indian company in 1953 and all the British employees left for Britain. Their bungalows and jobs as departmental heads were taken over by Indians. Over the next few years I saw their golf course turn into a grazing ground for cows and buffalos.

I quit the mill job in March 1952. However, I could not get a government job as I was still underage, so I continued peddling soap and other cleaning materials from village to village. My father's business did not progress too much, so the family also continued to live hand to mouth. Meanwhile, my elder brother Satpal got a job in the government's revenue department, based in a big village not very far from our town. His regular income helped the family buy new clothes and I too was able to buy a second-hand bike, which made my job as a pedlar easier.

In a life-changing stroke of good luck for me, the government brought out a scheme to recruit a large number of people to be trained as teachers for six months and then sent to villages all over India. I was selected for this training course and this guided the course of my life for many years to come.

3. THE BIRTH OF A TEACHER

I was appointed as a teacher in a village in March 1953, on completing the teacher-training course. I was given the responsibility of opening a new village school. It was still four months away from my eighteenth birthday, and I was keen and enthusiastic to do this job to the best of my abilities.

The village panchayat built two rooms for the primary school in an area surrounded by greenery and helped me to buy mats and books for the children. I also got a grant from the government to buy some simple furniture. I then started going from home to home, persuading parents to send their young children to the new school. The village elders helped me in this and within a month I had twenty children aged seven to eleven. Their numbers increased to 40 over the next two months. There were more boys than girls – about 30 boys and 10 girls . In most families, there was no tradition of educating girls. There was no tuition fee, although parents did have to pay for books. I found that these children were very eager to learn. The curriculum was limited to teaching the mother tongue, Punjabi, Hindi – the national language – and arithmetic. The mornings were for studying and the afternoons for reciting tables, games and drawing.

The main hurdle I faced was the children's poor attendance, as parents would often keep their children back for household chores. Parents did not give education priority. They felt that since the children were going to follow in their footsteps and become farmers, it wasn't of much use.

I found this job exhausting in the first six months, but then set a strict routine and much of the teaching became a manageable task. I nominated a few older boys and girls to be monitors and help me supervise various age groups.

There is a long-standing tradition in India of giving respect to teachers, so I never had discipline problems with the children. Although I placed a stick on my table as a deterrent, I hardly ever used it on any pupil during my three year stint.

I was also one of the few educated people in the village, which meant people would bring letters or government circulars to me. "Masterji, Masterji," their voices would call as I walked through the market, "can you read this for us please?"

Once I settled down into school, I felt a sharp desire to continue my own higher studies. I didn't just want to teach, I wanted to learn – but there was no evening college in my town. What to do?

Then, I happened to meet an ex-colleague who had successfully completed a degree course by studying privately at home. Aha! This gave me the inspiration to emulate his example and I began studying at home in the evenings. Three years later I gained my very first degree in English, History and Sociology from Punjab University. I also participated in additional teacher training courses during the summer breaks and got my final teaching certificate. Sweets were distributed all over my hometown the day the result came! Gaining a degree was no mean achievement! Can you imagine there were not more than five people in my town who had a degree at the time?

In the meantime my youngest brother Dharam was born and my sister Swaran got married at the tender age of sixteen.

My hunger for learning grew. I got admission at the newly started Graduate Teacher Training College in Mukatsar, in district Ferozepur, nearly 120 miles away from my town. I left my teaching job and went to Mukatsar with the financial support of my elder brother. I successfully completed this course and obtained a Bachelor of Education Degree from the Punjab University in September 1957 and was offered the post of Head Teacher in a middle school in the hilly area, 40 miles away from my home. It was a senior post and I was just 22 years old, but I got it because I already had three years of teaching experience behind me.

This job was hugely challenging as there were about 300 students, aged eleven to fourteen years, and twelve staff members all older than me – some even 55 years old! Here

When I achieved my first degree in 1956, at 21 years old

I was, a young man who came from the plains and couldn't even speak their mountain dialect!

Most of the people in the villages were illiterate orthodox Hindus whose main occupation was to plough small fields and look after their herds of sheep, goats, cows and buffaloes. Their main income came from selling wool and vegetables. The families all lived from hand to mouth. They lived simply and had no great aspirations for their children, as the custom was to take on your parent's occupation. The most difficult task for me was to motivate these children and parents. Most teachers had accepted that education was futile for the children as they were going to spend their adult life in the same village, earning their income in the exact same way as their forefathers. There were very few girls in this school too. I spent six months doing my best to change their attitude towards education, but I neither gained support from the other teachers, nor got very far. I started feeling very homesick and I left that job after completing my six-month contract.

I was offered a job in my old secondary school in Dhariwal and started working there, teaching History and English and preparing students for the matriculation examination.

Life moved on. My elder brother Satpal and my second sister Raj got married. I continued to help my father in my spare time, but his business never gained momentum. Mine and my elder brother's salary provided for the family. My younger brother completed his matriculation exam and got a clerical job at the Electricity Board in Patiala, a famous town in Punjab.

I kept feeling the desire to study more and more, in spite of not having much time as I was assisting my father in his business and my younger siblings in their education. Still, I persevered and received my Master's degree in History from Punjab University in 1960. I studied European history in the 1900s and learnt that the Indian army, work force and revenue played a very significant role in Britain's victory in both World Wars. I started to feel quite curious about this small island and wondered how its people were able to rule half the world. It was this fascination that grew and grew and finally brought me to the shores of the United Kingdom some years later.

My master's degree also helped me to secure a permanent teaching job in a prestigious government higher secondary school for boys. Funnily enough, the school was in Dera Baba Nanak – the town where I had stayed in a refugee camp with my family after the bloody Partition. It felt very strange to be back.

Memories of the camp, the confusion and the loss I had experienced at the time came rushing up. The town had changed a lot. It had been a prosperous town before the Partition. However, now that it was a border town, its make-up had changed. Soldiers from the nearby army brigade frequently visited it and most of its business community migrated to big cities like Delhi or Bombay. I saw a number of abandoned, ramshackle buildings tell this story over and over again. How people's lives had changed just because of religion!

Speaking of religion, the other interesting thing about Dera Baba Nanak was that it was an important place of worship, as a famous Sikh temple there had preserved a *chola*, an item of clothing worn by the first Sikh Guru, Baba Nanak Dev Ji.

I rented a flat there for the weekdays as it was 40 miles from my hometown, and I would bike back to my family every weekend.

With the blessings of the Almighty, the teaching post there was a good one. The school was big with over 1000 students. It was well equipped with science laboratories, art-craft rooms and a big library. Teachers came here from all over north India and the students came from the town and neighbouring villages and paid a small tuition fee that was affordable for most families.

I taught History to the top two classes at school and prepared them for the Higher Secondary Examination. I enjoyed this very much as the students were very keen to learn about India's past. I taught here for nearly four years. My students did well in their annual examinations and I was regarded as a strict but hard-working teacher who got the best out of his pupils.

Life seemed to have come full circle. I was back in the same place, where I had stepped foot in new India, traumatised and broken. Now, here I was, a successful, well-educated man who had conquered the impact of that terrible time and used it to grow from strength to strength.

4. THE DAY I MET PUSHPA

One day my mother said to me, "You are 25 years old, you have a good job, it's time you got married." She dusted the chapatti flour off her hands and that was that. My sister, who was married and living in Amritsar, teamed up with my mother and started putting pressure on me. "What kind of girl do you want, hmmm?" she asked teasingly. "I want a simple, domesticated girl who is not working and is like us," I replied. I left the finding and choosing of this girl up to them.

As it happened, Pushpa's family lived just two streets away from my sister's in Amritsar and they knew each other well. They too had migrated from the town of Narowal in Pakistan during the Partition. Pushpa had recently returned from her grandparent's house in Jammu, where she had lived and studied since she was seven. After passing her matriculation exam, she came back to Amritsar and started attending evening college there.

Pushpa's family agreed to pursue the matter after discussion with my sister and her family. Her two elder brothers and maternal uncle came to see me. Our families remained in informal contact, when much to our distress, my father took ill and had to be hospitalised in Amritsar. Pushpa's family used to visit my father regularly in hospital and this impressed him a lot. My father died in the hospital on the 3rd of January 1961 at just 52 years of age. He advised me to take the alliance forward before his passing.

His death was a terrible tragedy that affected our family irreversibly. The whole family was now dependant on my elder brother and me. My elder brother was already married and had one son, so I assumed full responsibility of my mother and three younger siblings.

My mother and sister finalised my betrothal with Pushpa and our marriage took place on the 9th of March 1962, one year after my father's death.

Now, here's the most interesting bit… All of my family had met Pushpa except for me! The first time I glimpsed her face was when she arrived at our house, *after* our marriage. Yes, after. So the day I first saw Pushpa was on our wedding day. This was quite common in arranged marriages in those days. When we told our children this story years later they found it very odd, but we assured them that although we had never met each other before our wedding, we were both traditionalists and believed in the sanctity and life-long nature of the marital relationship. There was no fashion of going on a honeymoon in those days, so after spending the weekend together, I returned to Dera Baba Nanak come Monday morning.

I would go back to see Pushpa and the family on weekends. We both tried to live together smoothly. My elder brother would also go on weekends to see his wife, son and the rest of the family. Nearly three months after mine and Pushpa's marriage, my mum persuaded my brother to move his wife and son to the place where he worked as his wife, my sister-in-law, was keen to go and live with him. I was pleased to notice that Pushpa was getting on very well with my mother and the rest of the family. She understood that she had to carry the family's responsibility with me 'til my siblings were able to stand on their own feet. She was good-natured and hardly ever complained to me on my weekly visits.

Our family was still living from hand to mouth, as there was only my salary, which had to fulfil everyone's needs. I could not afford to buy any new saris or ornaments for Pushpa, which all newly-married girls must expect from their husbands. In my heart of hearts, I kept worrying that she was suppressing all her desires and cursing me. Every weekend, I assured her that once we completed our responsibilities towards my younger siblings, I would satisfy all her needs for new clothes and jewellery. She never responded and in this way revealed her silent resentment, which I am afraid stayed with her all her life and came out from time to time during our many years of married life.

Wedding to my wife Pushpa in March 1962

In the October of 1963, a teacher training class for women started in a local girls' secondary school in Dera Baba Nanak, where I was working. I thought it was a good idea for Pushpa to enrol. The entire family now moved there and I rented a house big enough for us all.

Pushpa became pregnant with our first child as she started the course. She had a difficult pregnancy and had a very hard time coping with it whilst studying at the same time. The entire family rallied around her and gave her every possible support.

Indu Bala, our first child, was born on the 22nd of March 1963. We knew something was wrong, but we didn't know what it was. In the first few weeks her head was very soft. It only started hardening two months later. She was a very passive baby and hardly ever cried. All of her milestones were delayed – sitting up, crawling and walking. She would make noises, but they would form no coherent meaning. Later, once I'd moved to the UK, she was diagnosed with Downs Syndrome. It was a big shock to the family, as we had never seen a child with a similar condition in the family or town.

After four years in Dera Baba Nanak I wanted a promotion, so to increase my chances of getting one I pursued a masters in Education. I landed a senior teacher's post in a higher secondary school in Chandigarh, a modern town designed by a French architect. This town was the capital city of both Punjab and Haryana, and also the headquarters of the Punjab University. I started my job in Chandigarh in April 1964.

My younger brother was also in Chandigarh, working as a senior clerk in the electricity department. Fortunately, he was allocated a flat with his job, so I moved in with him, leaving Pushpa, Bala, my mother, two sisters and younger brother in Dera Baba Nanak. Whilst there, I started my masters in Education at the University College – a prestigious course that only accepted eight students in a year. When Pushpa passed her teacher-training course with good grades in March 1965, the family moved to Chandigarh. My sister Raksha gained admission into the teacher-training course in Gurdaspur and started her studies there.

Pushpa was soon pregnant with our second child and went to her parents' in Amritsar for the delivery. Our daughter Renu was born on the 13th of April 1965. I went to see her in Amritsar for two days. As I held Renu in my arms and looked down at her face, I thought: *What a lovely, smiling baby she is.* Pushpa came back to Chandigarh with our two young girls and joined the family in May 1965.

My masters course was a full-time one, so I gave private tuitions to two students in the evening to supplement the family income. It was a tough course with six essay papers and an advanced research project. I finished this course in September 1965, then re-joined my school and started earning my salary once again. I got my results after a month – I had passed with very good grades and was offered the option of studying part-time and completing a PhD. I agreed, but of course it was exhausting juggling a full-time job, looking after the family and studying.

In March 1966, I saw an advertisement in the newspaper that was going to alter the course of my life.

It was a posting by the UK Embassy advertising for teachers in the UK. I responded and was called for an interview at the Embassy, where I was granted a work permit for permanent employment in the UK then and there.

I discussed this offer with my university tutor who strongly advised me to take it up and apply to the Institute of Education at the University of London for my PhD. In his opinion a PhD from a London university would go a long way in getting me a professorship in one of the good Indian universities. At that time, a postgraduate degree from a university in London was greatly valued in the higher education departments in India.

I was very curious and tempted to take up the offer of the work permit. I wanted to see the UK and the educational establishments from which the English elite graduated and then went on to build the British Empire that ruled half the world!

The day I told my family about the work permit and my plans, there was a lull in the room. It seemed like the wind had stopped swishing and the birds had stopped twittering. Then the thunder broke – "Have you gone mad?" "Are you going to leave us and go?" "Have I brought you up to see this day?" My wife and mother expressed their opposition vociferously. My siblings joined in.

I wrote a letter to an ex-colleague, Mr. Duggal, who was now in the UK, teaching in Harlow, Essex. He wrote back to me, advising me not to come. *Conditions are not good for newly-arrived immigrants*, his letter said. *You have a very good position as a senior teacher in a reputable school and promising prospects for a career in higher education. Don't leave it.*

My desire to go to the UK did not diminish despite this. I kept thinking about it, kept imagining life over there. I also got a very encouraging reply to my application for a place on the post-doctoral course at the Institute of Education at the University of London . The days passed and there were only two weeks left before my work permit expired. I went back to my research tutor and finally decided. I was going to go.

Pushpa was inconsolable. Her friend had told her that people who went to London were entrapped by white women and left their wives behind in India forever. I tried and tried to allay her fears, but she wasn't convinced. Finally, I approached her parents. They encouraged her to trust and let me go as it would benefit the family in the long run. My mother asked me to reassure Pushpa that I will return to the family as soon as I complete my studies. My elder brother too asked for my promise to return. It was easy for me to give them these assurances as I had no plans to settle permanently in the UK at that point. Of course, I had no idea how life was going to unfold.

As the day I planned to leave drew closer, the tension in the family and inside me grew. On the one hand, I was excited and looking forward to this grand adventure, while on the other, anxiety and worry about an unknown future in an unknown country, far away from my loved ones, gnawed at me.

The one good thing that happened at that juncture was that the Director of Education in Punjab approved my leave of absence to study for a year. So, at least I knew I had my permanent job in India waiting for me in case I ran into bad luck in the UK.

My elder brother arranged the air ticket from Delhi to London. At last the day arrived – for me to leave my home, my country, my dearest mother, Pushpa, my two little girls

Before I first left India, with Renu, Bala and Pushpa

and family. I was allowed to carry three British pounds – the limit of foreign exchange you could take outside the country in those days. All my family came to Delhi Airport to say goodbye and bless me for my safe journey. Tears flowed from every eye. I tried to put on a brave face but could not help but sob when I took my two daughters into my lap and touched my mother's feet, seeking her blessings.

Although I was feeling the intense agony of leaving my family, job and country behind, I was also happy. I was finally fulfilling my childhood dream of going to the UK as well as my ambition of completing my higher education there.

I stepped into the waiting aircraft, flying on the wings of hope.

5. JOURNEYING INTO THE UNKNOWN

The 10th of July 1966 was the most memorable day of my life. Fear and sadness grappled with excitement and curiosity.

I had heard all about Delhi's airport, from where aeroplanes flew to different parts of the country and abroad, but that was the day I saw it for myself. I was going to fly in an aeroplane as a passenger for the very first time.

I went through a number of security checks. Both my body and luggage was scanned. My big suitcase was checked in and put on a conveyor belt that would take it to the aeroplane. Everything looked strange and new. I spent most of my time counting the arrival and departure of aeroplanes to keep my mind busy. The call to board brought the nail-biting wait to an end. I was feeling as excited as a child who gets his favourite toy and screams with happiness. I wanted to see what the aeroplane looked like inside. I was very curious about the cockpit as well. The airhostess welcomed the passengers and guided me to my allocated seat. I was very happy because I had a window seat, from which I would be able see everything when the aeroplane flew. I counted the number of windows and seats. All the seats were filled with passengers and the airhostess taught us how to put on our seat belts. I prayed for a safe journey to London before the flight took off at 8pm. I asked the airhostess lots of questions about flying and her experiences on the aeroplane. After one hour, we arrived in Bombay, our first stop. The flight to London would take off from here the next morning. Twenty passengers who were going to the UK, like me, were taken to a nearby hotel for the night.

I had read and heard a lot about this famous Indian city, the financial centre of the country and home to Bollywood stars, but had never seen it as it was nearly 1700 miles away from my hometown of Dhariwal.

The hotel was near the beach. I stood at the window watching the waves roll towards the shore, break and retreat in absolute amazement. What a beautiful scene it was! I had never seen the sea before, even though I had studied the oceans of the world. After dinner, I went to the beach for a walk. The silvery water lapped at my ankles. I bent and grazed it with my hands and tasted it. Salty! The new experiences I was seeking were coming to me one after the other and I was getting more and more excited.

Early the next morning, we were taken in a small bus to Bombay International Airport, where we boarded the flight for London. This was a much bigger aeroplane than the one that got us from Delhi! There were 150 passengers who were all going to London, and it took nearly eight hours for us to get there. It was a very tiring journey but I had the opportunity to talk to the airhostesses and some of the passengers who were going to the UK for the first time like me. Most of them had relatives who were already settled there, but I had no-one. I walked around the aeroplane and marvelled at how a small town boy's dream of travelling by air and going to the UK had finally come true.

At last, the flight landed at Heathrow Airport in London, safe and sound. It took me nearly two hours to get out of the airport, going through various checks, including immigration. The whole atmosphere looked very new, strange, somewhat complicated and frankly tiresome. For the first time in my life, I saw a few white porters helping passengers with their luggage trolleys. What a contrast to those two white men I'd seen in India, the big bosses; one in my father's office in Amritsar and the other in the woollen mill in Dhariwal!

Once out, I faced a big dilemma: *where should I go now?* I had just three British pounds in my pocket. I remembered a passenger at Delhi Airport telling me that I could use the three pounds to get a taxi to take me to the Southall Sikh temple, where they would help me with temporary boarding and lodging. As I was formulating this plan, I suddenly heard a voice calling my name. I cannot express the delight and relief I felt as I saw my best mate Mr. Duggal and his two friends there. He had obviously got the message of my arrival that I had sent him from Delhi. We hugged each other warmly. He and his friends hired a taxi and took me to his flat in Harlow, a new town in Essex where he was working as a teacher. All three had come from Punjab and asked me a number of questions about life back at home. They were living alone in different areas of the UK, waiting for the arrival of their families.

Everything was different in Duggal's two-bedroom flat. There was hot water, a bathtub and a toilet with a sink. The last two days were catching up with me – the emotions of leaving family, the new country and the uncertainty about the future. Duggal asked me to freshen up using the hot water in the bathtub. I finally felt somewhat rejuvenated after that. Having a safe place to stay and a warm welcome from my friend went a long way in building my confidence. I rang my family and assured them that I had arrived intact and would start working soon, hopefully.

Duggal had come to the UK on a work permit as a teacher, like me, in 1964. From our conversations, I realised that he'd had to endure a lot of problems before getting a teaching job. That was the reason he had discouraged me from coming. I spent two days in his flat after which he took me to the nearest social security office and I registered as a newly arrived immigrant in search of a teaching job. They gave me three pounds as my weekly allowance and offered me an interview with a local factory. As I listened to my friend's tough experiences, I slowly grasped that a teaching job was far away and I would have to accept any job that came my way, as I was in desperate need of money to send home to my brother to pay off the debt he had incurred from borrowing money to buy my air ticket. I accepted the job of unskilled labourer in a construction firm in Harlow, but could only survive two days there as the work was too tiresome for me.

There were very few Asians in Harlow and I began to feel very lonely. I contacted Mr. Bhandari, a friend in Southall, who invited me to his place and assured me that he would arrange some accommodation and work for me. After spending four days with Duggal I left for Southall, where most newly arrived immigrants from Punjab congregated. Bhandari had been my colleague while I was Head Teacher at a middle school, and he now gave me a very warm welcome. I felt at home in Southall, seeing the Indian shops, cinemas, pubs and restaurants. Bhandari arranged a job interview for me with a small factory in Hayes that made fishing rods. I got the job and was advised not to tell anyone about my post-graduate qualifications. I started working the 2-10pm shift. We were ten workers in all – two Indians and eight white people. The Indians huddled together and never mixed with the white workers during our tea breaks. The white workers occasionally made fun of our English and cracked jokes that we never understood.

I rented a box room, the smallest and cheapest room to rent in an Indian family's house. Thankfully, the landlady was kind enough to help me cook my food. Two weeks into the job, it dawned on me that not only was the job tiring, but the English workers spoke to us as if we were ignorant and uneducated, and showed no desire to interact with us. I felt no hope of getting a teaching job and felt excruciatingly lonely. I showed a brave face to Bhandari and my family, but when I shut the door to my bedroom, I would often cry.

I asked Bhandari to lend me some money, as I wanted to repay my brother as soon as possible. He very kindly lent me £100 and arranged for its delivery to my brother in Amritsar through the travel agent. Although the official value of the pound was thirteen rupees at the time, you could get up to 30 rupees via the travel agent. The travel agent gave 3000 rupees to my brother within two weeks of my arrival in the UK. My entire family was happy and astonished at my vast earnings.

I had a strange experience one weekend, soon after moving to Southall. My friend persuaded me to accompany him to an Indian Pub. I saw that a number of Indians were busy drinking alcohol, gambling and listening to Bollywood music. The room was full of smoke and the stench of drink. Bhandari got a pint of beer and persuaded me to have half of it. He too joined the others in playing cards, smoking and drinking. I found the environment suffocating, alien and immoral. The sip of beer, the smell of smoke and spirit all made my head dizzy. In India, especially as a teacher, I had never dreamt of buying a bottle of alcohol from a wine shop or drinking in public. It would have been absolutely immoral and socially unacceptable. My friend, however, explained to me that this was the way of life in England and they had all adapted to it. He assured me that I too would soon be quite accustomed to it. I left the pub half an hour later, returned to my box room and thought about this way of life for a very long time.

Days and weeks went by. It was my habit to ring my mother every Sunday morning. I would lie to her and tell her what a wonderful life I had. I would assure her that I would get a teaching job soon and start my further studies. However, after applying for various teaching positions I realised that my dream was a distant one. I was also finding the factory job tiring. As luck would have it, I passed the test for the job of a bus conductor with the London Transport Authority, followed by a fortnight-long training course. I became a fully-fledged bus conductor with the badge number *101894* and started working on the bus number 207, which ran from Ealing Broadway to Uxbridge bus station. I can never forget my start date, as it happened to be the 15th of August – the Indian Independence Day. I met many other bus conductors at my base, Uxbridge Bus Station, and realised that there were at least 30 others like me who had come to the UK on professional work permits, but had been unable to get work in their trained professions.

I started to enjoy this job. It wasn't as physically taxing as working at the factory and it also gave me the opportunity to practice speaking English in an English accent. I roamed the city, taking in historic and cultural sights thanks to the free bus pass I received.

I made friends with another Indian colleague, who like me was keen to land a teaching position. We would buy the *Times*

With the Godolphin School staff, Slough, 1968

Educational Supplement and apply for five to six jobs every week. After sending as many as 95 job applications, I got one hopeful response. I was called for an informal interview at the Slough (Berkshire) Education Office.

The 22nd of November, 1966. This is a significant date in my diary. An education officer took me to a primary school to meet with the Head Teacher. I hoped that I would be fortunate enough to get a teaching job in that school. In the mean time, I also clinched two more interviews for teaching jobs – one for Hertfordshire County Council and the other for a London Borough. I didn't get either of those jobs, but I was asked to come back to the Slough Education Office on the 14th of December 1966, this time for a formal interview. They offered me a job for one term only, and so it was on the 4th of January 1967 that I started at Godolphin Junior School.

The headmaster was Mr. Spink – a nice gentleman who had experience of teaching in a foreign country, which made him sympathetic to the difficulties I faced professionally as a foreigner with a different accent. He advised me to speak very slowly so that the children would be able to understand me and used me as a supply teacher, which gave me the experience of teaching three different age groups. Mr. Spink was impressed by my practical teaching methods and advised the Education Officer to extend my contract by another term.

Meanwhile, a number of newly arrived immigrant children of various age groups arrived from the Indian Subcontinent and were admitted into the school. They needed intensive coaching in learning to speak, read and write in English. Mr. Spink, in consultation with the Education Office, decided to start a special class for them and put me in charge of it. He also assigned an English lady as my assistant. I had twenty children between the ages of seven and ten who had recently arrived from India, and I was able to communicate with them effectively as well as build their confidence, since I could speak three Indian languages.

I realised that these children were suffering abuse and rejection from the white children every day, which is why they stuck together in their own groups during playtime and after school. This made my job of teaching them English rather difficult. Even so, I met the parents of these children, with the help of the Head Teacher, and sought their co-operation in helping the children practice speaking English after school hours. Some of the children made good progress in just one term. The Education Officer came to inspect my classes twice during that term and I hoped that I would get a permanent teaching contract from the Borough Council after the expiry of my temporary one.

In June 1967, I was offered a permanent contract as a teacher in the Slough Borough Council. I was the first Asian teacher to be given one by them.

In the meantime, two very important events occurred in my life. My younger sister, Raksha, got married in February 1967 and I was not able to attend this significant celebration and give her my blessings for a long and happy married life in person. I spent the whole day and night calling home and crying my eyes out.

The other major event was the arrival of Pushpa with my younger daughter Renu in April 1967. Sadly, she had to leave Bala, our elder daughter, behind with my mother as I was having a lot of trouble getting accommodation for the four of us. On my salary I could only hire one bedroom, which was not big enough for four of us. There was also a lot of hatred directed towards immigrants due to colour prejudice in those days, and it was just not possible to rent from a local white family.

Pushpa's arrival helped in alleviating some of my loneliness and emotional tension. It was lovely to go home and play with my little Renu after a hard day's work at school. At the same time, my head teacher Mr. Spink encouraged me to follow my dream of pursuing my higher education.

In August 1967, I was granted an interview with a professor called Mr. Foss at the Institute of Education. He advised me to pursue a master's degree from the Institute before registering for a PhD, and offered me a place as a part-time student. There were twelve students on the course, including three Indians. The main subject of study was Educational Psychology. The assignments included four essay papers and a dissertation project.

We were hard-pressed for money and Pushpa had to take up a part-time job at a local sweet factory while a child minder looked after Renu. We didn't just need money to furnish our home and live our day-to-day lives, but also to send back to my mother and younger siblings in India. We could not afford any new furniture for the house, so looked for second hand items. Those were hard times for us. I would leave home at 8am for school and rush to the railway station at 4pm after it finished to go to the Institute of Education in London. The journey was an hour and a half long. I would study from 6pm to 9pm and then return home by 10 or 11pm. Pushpa would wait for me so that we could have our dinner together, but I hardly got to see Renu on weekdays. On many Saturdays I had to go to

Pushpa, Bala and Renu coming to England

the Library and prepare my assignments. I would come back in the afternoon and we would do our weekly shopping.

Bala joined us in April 1968, when the Council gave us a three-bedroom house. We were glad for it, as three people in one bedroom, sharing the kitchen and bathroom with the Indian landlady and her family had become increasingly difficult. The landlady had imposed a number of restrictions on our movements around the house, which had made us feel suffocated. I shared the situation with Mr. Spink, who helped us get the three-bedroom house from the Council.

We were the first Asian family who got a house in this all-white council estate, and I don't think that Pushpa and I can ever forget our first three months there. We had to suffer all sorts of abuse, not just from children but also from teenagers and adults. They gave us dirty looks and made racial comments whenever they saw us. Three times, people threw stones and smashed our bedroom window. A terrified Pushpa begged me, "Please, please let's go back to India!" She could not bear this humiliating and fearful situation. I kept telling her that the moment I fulfilled my ambition of completing my PhD, we would go back. In three months, we endured 35 incidents of stone and muck throwing and abuse. I managed to stick it out with the support of Mr. Spink and our two neighbours. The neighbours were an older couple from Wales and often chased away youngsters when they threw stones at our house. The Head Teacher approached the local police inspector who organised special patrols in our street. He and his wife also invited us over for tea at their house and helped in building Pushpa's confidence.

Bala was four years old when she came, but she could not speak and was very slow in her movements. I took her to Great Ormond Street Hospital for a proper diagnosis of her physical and mental condition. After six months of regular testing, we were told that she had Downs Syndrome and would need a special education from a special school. Bala started her special school in the September of 1968 and Renu was offered a part-time place in the nursery at the Godolphin Infants School.

These two years from October '67 to July '69 were the most difficult and busy ones in my life. The day started with putting Bala onto her school bus, taking Renu with me to the nursery class, attending my full-time teaching job, going to the station from the school, catching a train to Paddington station, changing lines and getting to Euston Square to go to the Institute of Education. Pushpa remained very busy as well, looking after two young girls, doing her part-time job and managing the household.

I worked hard at school, giving the newly arrived children intensive one-to-one coaching in speaking English. My assistant, a middle-aged lady, also showed a keen interest in teaching them. Some children made such good progress that they were transferred to the main class in only a few months. During my two and a half years teaching this special class, none of the children became capable of passing the 11+ examination, but they did become proficient in the use of the English language and managed to integrate into the main classes.

Except during the short daily recess, I did not have much contact with the other staff at the school. It felt like most of the other teachers did not think very much of my teaching qualifications from India, and never involved me in any activities that could encourage the immigrant children to mix with the others. Perhaps they were prejudiced or perhaps they

My Masters Graduation Ceremony, Institute of Education in London, 1969

did not understand the educational background that both the children and I came from.

I started applying for other teaching jobs in September 1969, and was selected by the London Education Authority for a three-month training course for teaching children with special needs. Before leaving my teaching job in Slough, the Education Officer invited me over and commended my work. He told me that my practical teaching skills and my devotion to the children had encouraged him to offer teaching jobs to ten other immigrant teachers in various schools in Slough. I felt really proud at that moment – my teaching competence had given the Education Officer the confidence to offer permanent job contracts to my countrymen!

I took my written examination for my MA and submitted my dissertation. I graduated from the London university in October 1969. I also passed my driving test after two attempts. Travelling around town became easier after that and I bought an old car for £50 to do so.

There were nineteen teachers on the Special Education Teacher Training Course with me, though I was the only one from a BAME background. All the teachers who took this training were placed in various special schools after one term, except for me. The Education Office admitted that they were having problems placing me because of my immigrant background. They sent me to teach in the Stamford Remand Home for Young People in the Borough of Hammersmith instead.

This had to be the most challenging experience of my entire teaching career. The Remand Home was a place where young offenders were sent before being sent to Court to be put on trial for their offences. It was a residential establishment and there was a head teacher, six other teachers, an educational psychologist, a psychiatrist nurse, social workers, probation officers, cooks and security staff there. There were fifteen young people in each class and there were six classes in total. Security would lock us in our classrooms with the teenagers. We had to keep them busy from 9am to 12-noon and then again from 1 to 4pm. These children had mostly had a poor experience of school life and hated all authority figures. They spent their time playing games, doing craftwork and drawing. They were allowed to watch some educational programmes on the television. There was no morning assembly or any collective physical activity. There was no real teaching, just containment.

I can never forget their regular chanting as they watched a police car bringing in more young people to the centre: "Coppers are bastards. Coppers are bastards." They wouldn't stop chanting 'til the police van disappeared and no threats from teachers and security staff worked.

It was difficult to establish any sort of relationship with these children and I was always on my toes because of my immigrant status. There was also always the fear that one of these teenagers would lose his temper and become violent. They had deep emotional and social problems and had come from backgrounds where education wasn't valued. I stayed there from January to July 1970 and learnt a lot about these young delinquents. Most of them seemed to be the victims of their circumstances – children from broken homes and unsocial environments. Our schools and education system had failed them. The knowledge that I gained there proved very useful to me when I became an educational psychologist.

In September 1970, I was transferred to the Elizabeth Burgwin Special Secondary School for children with moderate learning difficulties. I worked there for nearly four years and was promoted to the post of Grade B Teacher, with the responsibility of assessing children's progress, after a year. I really enjoyed teaching at this well-established special school. All the teachers including the Head Teacher were very supportive of the children and each other. I was the only teacher from a BAME community (black, Asian, minority ethnic background) but did not feel any discrimination from any member of the staff – perhaps because I was the most highly-qualified teacher in the school.

During my four-year stint I noted one very significant change in the demographic of children attending this school. In 1970 only 5% of the children were from black families, but by the time I moved on in 1974, their numbers had grown to nearly 60% of the school's intake. This showed a rapid demographic change in the population of London.

On assessing the children, I found that a large number were wrongly placed in this special school. The reason for this was obviously racial. Finding their behaviour in the classroom to be a problem, the white teachers sent them to this special school, taking advantage of the fact that their parents had no idea about the school system in this new country. As most developing countries – whether in the West Indies or the Indian Subcontinent – did not have this type of special school, awareness about them amongst parents was quite low. Fortunately, I was able to send a few children back to the mainstream schools, working hard alongside the Educational Psychologist and the parents.

The Head Teacher had an interesting bit of trivia to share with me in this regard. He told me that he had been working in this school for over twenty years, and when he had just started, the school had been full of Irish children. At that point it was the Irish who were the newly arrived immigrants and they too had suffered the sort of discrimination that Asians and black immigrants were suffering now.

Coming back to my progress in my studies, I registered for a PhD in March 1970 at the Institute of Education. I was allocated a tutor who approved my research project – a comparative study of the educational aspirations of black,

Holding my son Rajesh outside 44 Hutton Avenue

Asian and English children studying in London schools. I started working on it with great enthusiasm and would spend three to four hours after school at the research library at the Institute of Education. I did all of my background research in the first year itself and prepared an outline for collecting data. I chose five secondary schools in London and one in Southall.

My son Rajesh was born nearly a year later in February 1971. Pushpa and I were overjoyed. It was the happiest day of our lives as we had been praying for a son. We named him Raj. He was a handsome and healthy baby. Pushpa left her part-time job to look after our three children.

In front of the Taj Mahal with Raj

My workday would start at 8am and finish by 11pm, so I hardly had any time for my lovely son and my two young daughters. Simultaneously, my PhD research tutor was not very helpful and tried to persuade me to go back to India. I was very stressed and decided to postpone my research project and give more time to my son and two young daughters. The educational psychologist at my school also advised me to try my luck training as an educational psychologist. He convinced me that four years of hard work towards a PhD would not really advance my career in the UK.

My family

In December that year, I finally went back to India with my little boy and two girls and met my family after a span of five long years! What a joyous reunion it was! I discussed my situation with my mother and elder brother and they agreed that I should postpone my PhD studies and concentrate on bringing up my young family. It was the death knell to my lifelong ambition of becoming a Doctor of Philosophy.

On my return to the UK, I started applying for a place in some prestigious Educational Psychology courses. Admissions were quite difficult as there were only 100 places in all. I was also an immigrant, which made it even harder for me to get in. I applied for two places in the April of 1972, but did not get called for an interview. I carried on undeterred and finally was offered a place at a college in Swansea, part of the University of Wales. I do think the fact that my interviewer, Professor Chazan, came from a minority community – Jewish in this instance – helped my case. I successfully completed this postgraduate training course, achieving a distinction in my research project. I bid goodbye to twenty-one years of a career in teaching and set foot on a new path as an educational psychologist.

It was seven years since I had first set foot in the UK – a small town boy who had flown across the seas to fulfil his dreams. My dreams met a harsh reality, but in the process I learnt that I had a strength and grit that I had not imagined. The success I achieved was far sweeter for it.

6. I CAN AND I WILL

Then began a new phase of my life and career. In September 1973, I started my postgraduate degree in Educational Psychology at the Ponty Pridd campus of the University of Wales, Swansea.

I hired a room in an elderly lady's house in Gower, the old part of the city, where a large number of residents spoke the Welsh language. I soon realized that everyone here was very welcoming and friendly, a sharp contrast to the people of London. The local shopkeeper from whom I would buy my groceries would trust me to pay him later on in the week if I was short of cash. People on the street smiled and responded to me when I wished them 'Good morning' or 'Good evening'. This was such a pleasant change to the attitude of the people in London and Slough towards immigrants, and I will always remember this place fondly for this reason.

I began my course with great enthusiasm. The course at Ponty Pridd was highly regarded in the UK. They also had other courses to provide training to postgraduate teachers and school counsellors. Our lectures often overlapped so that we could familiarise ourselves with various roles. The course consisted of monthly assignments, practical training, and the development of our skills in assessment and interviewing via role-play, counselling and research.

There were nine students in my class, two women and seven men. Five of them were taking a four-year course, which included a year of teacher training, two years of teaching experience and a final year of training as an educational psychologist. There were four of us who had joined them in that final year. All four of us were mature students with a fair amount of experience in teaching and other related occupations under our belts.

The course was intensive and demanding, and I started feeling the strain of it in the first week. I found the subject matter difficult, the classroom discussions tough to comprehend and the question and answer sessions too fast to follow. I was very conscious that my accent was different to everyone else's and that kept me from participating in classroom discussions. An inferiority complex gripped me and I started feeling that the other eight trainees were much brighter than I was.

Two weeks later, I came home and dejectedly told Pushpa, "This course is too hard for me. I don't know how long I will be able to continue, so there goes my ambition of becoming an educational psychologist." After that initial outburst, I spent all weekend reflecting and encouraging myself. I finally made up my mind. I was going to work as hard as was needed to succeed in this course.

My tutor, Professor Maurice Chazan, must have picked up on my earlier depressed mood because he called me into his room for a discussion on my research project when I returned. I spent half an hour explaining my research topic to him and also shared my difficulty in coping with the course and my concerns about it. He listened patiently and at the end said just two sentences, "Yash, you are very capable. I have full confidence in your abilities and I know that you will fulfil all the demands of this course." I felt like I had been rescued.

The meeting really boosted my morale and I worked hard on my first written assignment. At the same time, I also made friends with two others on the training course – one was a mature person of my age and experience in life and the other was a bright young man from a Jewish background. We had long discussions about our life experiences, the course and the field of education. This went a long way in building my confidence, but I have to say, the biggest bolster was the A grade I got on my first assignment. From that day onwards, I started participating in class discussions and in question and answer sessions. It felt like the other students showed a more empathetic understanding of my accent and speech then.

I went home to Pushpa and the children every other weekend to spend time with them and help her out. We'd do a big shop for groceries and other things that were needed for the children. Pushpa was working very hard, running the household singlehandedly and managing the demands of a growing family. Soon after Christmas, coursework became hectic and intense and I could only make monthly visits home. Thankfully, Pushpa and the children coped very well without me. The pressure didn't ease off until June 1974.

On the 15th of June 1974, Pushpa had an accident while crossing the road and had to be admitted to hospital. I got to know of it when Renu rang me crying. I immediately informed my tutor, dropped everything and left for Slough to see her. She was discharged the next day with a bandage to support her arm. I had to return to Swansea on the 19th of June 1974 for a short while, for an interview with the external examiner. However, as most of my course had finished, my tutor allowed me to stay home and finish my dissertation. I returned to Swansea to submit my dissertation at the end of June 1974 and said goodbye to everyone there.

I was delighted with my exam result when I got it – a distinction in my research dissertation. I also got a wonderful testimonial from my tutor Professor Maurice Chazan. I remember him with utmost respect. He is my professional Guru.

I enjoyed my time in Swansea city, an ancient coastal town. It had a lovely beach, many opportunities for higher education, but most of all warm-hearted people. The city's population was about 200,000 at that time and the Asian population made up just 1% of this. The Asians here were mainly professionals working in health and education. A psychologist called Mr. Verma supervised my training at the Swansea Child Guidance Clinic. Like me, he had come from

India on a teacher's work permit and had got a job in Wales. We became very close friends and remained so until his sad death in 2008.

Since I knew how difficult it was for immigrants to get professional jobs, I started applying for educational psychologist roles in the first term of my training course itself. I applied for two jobs, one in Berkshire and the other in Essex in November 1973. I didn't get any reply from Berkshire but the Essex Education Department called me for an interview on the 20th of December 1973. The interview took place at County Hall in Chelmsford. Two hours and a presentation later, they offered me a job, conditional to the successful completion of my course.

I was absolutely thrilled! I was the first trainee on the course to get of a permanent job offer. Everyone was surprised, but they all congratulated me. I was highly motivated and worked extremely hard to complete my training successfully. I personally thanked Professor Chazan for his support. Later, I learnt that my interviewer was an alumnus of the Swansea training course and had a high regard for it.

I was offered a permanent contract for the job upon completing my course, and started at the Thurrock Child Guidance Clinic from the 1st of August, 1974.

In July, before I started, the Principal Psychologist promised to help me get a council house, as I was not in a position to sell my house in Slough. On the 15th of July 1974, I came to Grays with Pushpa and the children to pick up the keys to our council house and to walk around the town and get more familiar with it.

I also went over to the Grays Child Guidance Clinic to have a look at it and met the Senior Psychologist and the other administrative staff. The Senior Psychologist was a young lady who gave me the impression that she was not happy with my appointment. I later learnt that she was putting pressure on the Principal Psychologist to send me to Castle Point Child Guidance Clinic and allow one of her friends to come to Grays instead.

On the 29th of July 1974, we left Slough with tears in our eyes. We had stayed there seven years and had made a few close friends, mostly Indians. In Slough, nearly 20% of the population was made up of immigrants, mostly from the Indian Subcontinent.

While Slough was a modern town, Thurrock was an ancient one. It had a long history that went back to Roman and Saxon times. The Peasant's Revolt had started there, from a small village called Fobbing. Queen Elizabeth I gave her famous Armada Speech from Tilbury Fort. The East India Company used the Port of Tilbury for the import and export of goods. Most Indians, who came to the United Kingdom by ship, docked at this port first. The famous Empire Windrush, with the first batch of immigrants from the West Indies, had anchored here. More recently, the famous film *Four Weddings and a Funeral* was shot at St Clement's Church in West Thurrock. Perhaps it's this history that made Thurrock welcoming to immigrant families, even though they made up of only 2-3% of the population when we made it our home.

Our three-bedroom council house was in Chadwell St. Mary, nearly two miles from Grays town centre. It took us about a week to settle in. There were a few council houses on this quiet street and we didn't encounter problems of the sort that we had when we moved into the council house in Slough. Our neighbours were friendly and our children soon started playing with the next-door neighbours' children, who were about the same age as them.

I started at Grays Child Guidance Clinic. There were ten staff members in all – three educational psychologists, one psychiatrist, one psychiatric social worker, one remedial adviser and four clerical staff. I was the only one from the BAME community and it was a new experience for the staff. The team was a multi-disciplinary one that worked together to help children and families with social and emotional problems.

The main work of the educational psychologist was to provide psychological support to children with special needs in 65 local schools and ten special units – nearly 25,000 children. I was responsible for 25 of those schools and two units.

I started my job in August, when the schools were closed. I was looking forward to working with the children, but was also apprehensive as this was a very different job to that of a teacher. As a psychologist, I would have to deal with problem children from problem families in a mainly white population. I feared the hostility that I might have to face as an immigrant. Adding to my ambivalence was the fact that my speech was still tinged with an Indian accent and I spoke the Queen's English, which was very different to the local dialect.

The Senior Psychologist, who was my immediate boss, was not very amicable. Thankfully, I established a good rapport with my secretary and colleague Malcolm. Through August, I had the opportunity to go through the files of all my 25 schools and two units. The Principal Psychologist also came to welcome me to Essex and assure me that I had his support in establishing myself. This in itself was very encouraging and confidence-bolstering.

There were three lessons I had learnt by then and these stood me in good stead. They were:

Listening to others is more important than speaking.

Thorough preparation is more important than delivering.

To compete with local white colleagues, I have to work twice as hard as them — set work targets and push myself to achieve them

I felt that since I had been reasonably successful in my teaching jobs and on my training course, I could also make my mark in this challenging but prestigious job in the education department.

I visited all my schools and units between September and December 1974 and received a warm welcome from most head and senior teachers. I also met all 25 educational psychologists at the County meeting in December 1974. Again I was the only psychologist from the BAME community as well as a first generation immigrant. I listened carefully to the Principal Psychologist and the Chief Inspector, a guest speaker at this meeting. Both of them came up to me and inquired about my family's adjustment in Thurrock. I assured them that we were all happy and settling down well. Renu and Bala had already

With the Essex team of psychologists, 1974

started their respective schools and Raj had got a place in a nursery unit attached to the Tilbury Infant School.

Renu was the only Asian child in her whole school. After attending school for a few days, I noticed that she was reluctant to go. I asked if she was having any kind of problems, but she said nothing. One day she started to cry and told me that a big boy in her school would swear at her and make racially abusive comments whenever she passed by. Poor thing was scared to tell the teacher.

I went with her to school the very next day and met the Head Teacher about this. He was very concerned and assured both Renu and me that he would deal with the boy and talk to his parents immediately. He told her that she should tell him if he ever bothered her again. That was the only incident of racial bullying that my children suffered in any of their schools in Thurrock that I can recall.

After spending one term at my job, I realised that I should be doing more to establish myself as a successful educational psychologist, not just in the schools but also in the county. This desire guided my progress in my career.

I decided to visit my schools regularly – at least once a month – and assured all the head teachers that I would respond to their phone calls within 24 hours and offer appointments to referred children within a week. This was a novel move on my part as there used to be a waiting time of three to four months for a child to be seen by the psychologist after his/her referral. In just one term, I reduced it to one month. Because of my long teaching experience I was also able to understand the problems teachers were facing while dealing with children who had special needs. In just two terms, I started to feel a sense of confidence. I established myself and gained the respect of the head teachers and class teachers.

During my third term in Thurrock, we started looking for a house. We found a three-bedroom terraced house near the town centre, which fulfilled most of our needs and was affordable. We sold our house in Slough and bought this house in Grays. After a year in the council house, we moved into our new home in August 1975.

My mum came to spend four months with us after years of me asking. She was keen to see where and how we lived, spend some time with the children and see with her own eyes how I was bringing them up without her supervision.

At the same time, Pushpa started working full-time at Bata Shoe Company in East Tilbury, as we needed extra money to furnish our new house. A number of Asian women were already working there and she felt quite comfortable in their company. An Indian driver would pick them up and take them to the factory at 8am and bring them back at 5pm.

It was now my responsibility to take children to their respective schools and make arrangements for their return. Renu had to change schools and started at Quarryhill Junior School, While Raj started at Quarryhill Infants School. Bala attended a special school and would take the school bus. Life was very busy for Pushpa and me. For a few months, Mum

My mother with her grandchildren during her visit to the UK

helped me to get the children ready for school in the mornings and to bring them back as well.

We took my mother to many places so that she could enjoy her holiday and meet all of our friends and relatives in England. She was very pleased to see us living happily and working hard. She was also very impressed by the cleanliness of the streets and the honesty of the shopkeepers. After spending four months with us, she started feeling homesick and wanted to go back to Dhariwal, where her large family and friends awaited. When she got a letter from my youngest sister saying that she was not feeling too well, Mum made up her mind. She would leave as soon as we would arrange her ticket back to Amritsar. We bid her goodbye with heavy hearts on the 12th of December 1975 at Heathrow Airport. Those four months were the happiest time of my life since I had arrived in the UK.

I now started my second year on the job with a sense of self-assurance. I had established a good rapport with my schools and two special units. I began to think bigger. I started thinking of ways and means by which I could gain professional recognition, not just amongst my colleagues in Essex, but in the country.

With my mother

I had a good grounding in and knowledge of research techniques. So I decided to initiate some useful research projects with the help of the teachers and head teachers of my schools and units. These projects would train teachers to try new teaching methods that could improve the children's achievements and behaviour.

The first project started in one of my special units where children with some learning difficulties were withdrawn from their schools and given intensive coaching to enhance their basic literacy skills. We started an evaluation project that measured their achievements during their stay in this withdrawal unit.

This project continued for nearly two years and the findings were published in Essex Education (1977) Vol. 3 No. 3 under the heading *"A Psychologist's work with a withdrawal group in Thurrock"*. This paper was distributed amongst all the psychologists and the inspectors in Essex.

In the same year, another paper was published in the British Journal of Sociology (1977) vol. XXV111 No. 2, pages 185 to 198, under the heading *"The Educational and Vocational Aspirations of Asian Immigrant and English School Leavers"*. This paper was based on the findings of my research project at the training course for educational psychologists at Swansea.

At Grays Child Guidance Clinic, I was working in harmony with all my colleagues from other disciplines. As it happened, my boss, the Senior Psychologist, went on maternity leave and finally decided to quit her job. This gave me the perfect opportunity to try my luck and seek her position. After an interview, competing with two other psychologists, I was lucky to clinch it in February 1977 after working as an educational psychologist for just two and half years.

It was never going to be easy for an immigrant coming from the Indian Subcontinent to be accepted as the boss.

One of the people who had been in the running for the job with me was a psychologist from Grays Clinic. He was very disappointed to not get the job and his feelings of jealousy were quite apparent on his face. He undermined my authority from day one. He adopted a very clever approach, which was to say yes to everything I asked him to do, but then not do it. I found it highly frustrating, but could not think of a solution to the problem. The absence of the Senior Psychologist meant that the both of us had to share her workload as well, which was crushing. My colleague's negative attitude was also rubbing off on two of the administrative staff. The new post became a bed of thorns, but I was determined to turn it into the success story of my life.

From my previous experience of working with a white assistant while I was a class teacher, I had learnt that I should keep smiling and never lose my cool. All I can say is that it was very difficult for me to smile while my colleagues in the clinic were determined to challenge my authority and were not cooperating.

Finally, I spoke to the Principal Psychologist and asked him to come over and have a word with this colleague and the administrative staff. He had a one to one with my colleague. Everyone assured me of their cooperation moving forward. Fortunately, within a month of this meeting, my colleague got a job with another authority and I heaved a sigh of relief.

We appointed two new psychologists with the help of the Principal Psychologist. I now had a full staff and was raring to go in my new role as the Senior Psychologist, responsible for delivering efficient service to local schools and special units. It took nearly six months and during this time I came to three significant conclusions:

1. Never lose your cool and never let inside anger show on your face, ever.
2. Keep smiling and have a positive attitude towards difficult people and situations. This was totally against my nature, but I reigned in my strong negative emotions with discipline.
3. Never talk about one colleague to another. Keep your feelings to yourself, rather than sharing them with the staff.

Looking back now, I can see that I was very insecure and fearful of losing my authority and even my job. I felt that no one would stand by me if I made a mistake. The fear was real, as I knew of an Asian teacher who had been promoted to

Deputy Head in a primary school and then lost his job within six months because of his temperament.

Outside of the clinic, the teachers and head teachers had a mixed reaction to me. The head teachers in my own area were positive about my appointment, whereas the other head teachers expressed concerns about my ability to manage the district. These feelings were voiced when I attended the termly meeting of head teachers with the Education Officer for the first time. They criticized the lack of psychological services to their schools and I was asked about my plans to improve this. I did so and was supported by the Education Officer.

As a psychologist, I built a good relationship with two of the head teachers who were in good standing amongst their colleagues. They both came from Wales and regularly supported my work as the Senior Psychologist. I would consult with them about my plans and my research projects and benefitted from their positive inputs. My faith in God and my confidence in my own abilities helped me to establish myself as a valuable psychologist and a good administrator.

I continued my professional growth and joined a part-time two-year evening course at Birbeck College in London where I learnt the use of consultation techniques. This course helped me start two support groups – one for senior teachers and the other for head teachers at Grays Child Guidance Clinic. The groups met once a week after school and discussed professional issues that they faced in their day-to-day jobs.

While these meetings were helpful to all participating teachers, they were equally useful to me in enhancing my image as a senior psychologist in the district and the county. I published three research articles in various educational journals based on my work with these groups, which brought me national recognition as a Senior Psychologist. These were:

"Some observations after two years group work with teachers in Thurrock" Therapeutic Education (1978) Vol. 6 No. 2, pp 16-22.

"Support Group for Thurrock Secondary School Teachers" Essex Education (1982) Vol. 35 No. 2.

"Head teachers too need Pastoral support." Educational Psychology in Practice (1985) Vol. 1 No. 3.

In the meantime, I also carried out some other research work on various educational issues and published my findings in various national educational journals:

"Behavioural Problems in an EPS school in Essex" Therapeutic Education (1978) Vol. 6 No. 2, pp 12-20.

"The roles of the Educational Psychologist as seen by a Group of Psychologists and Head teachers." Links (1980) Vol. 6 No. 1, pp 17-21.

"Identification of Infant Children with Poor Learning Skills." Remedial Education (1981) Vol. 16 No. 16, pp 137-142.

"Some problems in the Identification of the Intellectually Bright Infant Children." LINKS (1980) Vol. 5 No. 2, pp 22-28.

"The Children with Epileptic Fits; Some facts and observations." LINKS (1985) Vol. 10 No. 2, pp 12-15.

"Gifted Children in our Schools – Their identification and Education." LINKS (1985) Vol. 10 No. 3, pp 9-14.

"Group Counselling Sessions at a Comprehensive School in Thurrock." By Y. Gupta & J. Ayres. Essex Education (1985) pp 5-8.

"Teaching Spellings." By S. Bayley, Y. Gupta & J. Bold. Perspectives (1985) Vol. 1 No. 5, pp 8-11.

During my career as an educational psychologist I wrote as many as 32 research articles and ten book reviews, which were published in various national research journals. A list of these publications can be found in the appendix.

I also led a group of Essex psychologists to formulate a county policy document on promoting equal opportunities. I offered my services to any psychologist in Essex who needed help assessing children from the Indian Subcontinent who were not proficient in English, but spoke Hindi, Punjabi or Urdu – languages that I was well versed in. Only two psychologists, one from Harlow and the other from Colchester, took me up on this. While working as Senior Psychologist in Thurrock, I set up a local multi-professional group that we called the Personal Services Group. Its main purpose was to share information about any project or development in any department with those working for local communities, especially with children and their parents. In October 1983 I was elected Chair of this group. We would meet once a month, during lunchtime — from 1 to 2pm.

Some of us from this group went on to set up Thurrock Mind, a voluntary organisation which would provide support and help to those suffering from mental illness. Thurrock Mind has been a great success over the years and I continue to support this very valuable organisation. The second voluntary organisation that I got involved in was Thurrock Open Door. It was set up by teachers and youth workers to provide help and support to young people between the ages of eleven and eighteen. These were mainly children who came from dysfunctional families and had problems in school.

In 1986, the Essex Education Department was restructured. Thurrock and Basildon were merged and called South West Essex. Once again, I had to compete for the job of Senior Educational Psychologist within the new structure and was very pleased when I got it. There was no increase in salary but my responsibilities increased manifold.

After my appointment as Senior Psychologist in Thurrock, I realised that I had reached the peak of my professional career and was going to be in this position for a long time. Salary and status-wise, this job was equivalent to a Group 9 secondary head teacher.

Pushpa and I started to look for better accommodation for our family – a place where each of our children could have their own bedroom. We preferred a house closer to the town centre, which would give Pushpa easy access to the shops and

With all of my brothers at Renu and Akhil's wedding

me the library. We liked a newly built detached four-bedroom house very close to the town centre. I went to see the estate agent and expressed my interest. It was a very expensive property, twice the price of a regular three-bedroom house. The estate agent took one look at me and told me that it had been sold. I just knew he was lying. Of course, the reason was racial discrimination, but I said nothing and went back to the clinic.

My secretary saw the disappointment and anger on my face, as I had discussed my keenness to buy this house with her. She brought me a soothing cup of tea. I sipped at it,

Raj's Graduation

feeling at a loss and not knowing what to do. She came back after half an hour later and offered to speak to the agent. She told me that she had worked as a secretary for the head of that real estate firm before getting the job in the clinic. I was very happy for her help.

She went to see the head of the agency and told him a little about me, my job and my disappointment at the behaviour of his staff member. The man rang me and expressed his regret. He then fixed a meeting with me, during which we finalised the deal for this house. He also told me that his colleague had simply assumed that I would not be able to afford such an expensive house as most immigrants could only afford houses in the cheaper areas of the borough. This house, in contrast, was situated on a more exclusive street, where there were no other immigrant families.

We moved into our new home on the 20th of January, 1978. We named it *THE PUSHAP* just to please Pushpa Ji, and have been living here happily ever since. Our three children decorated their bedrooms in their own way.

Renu went from Quarry Hill Juniors to Grays Comprehensive School where she passed her O Level examination and attended Thurrock College of Further Education to complete her A Levels. She took up a temporary job with the Job Centre and liked it so much that she continued working there even after her marriage to Akhil, a dental technician, on the 2nd of July 1988. Her marriage to Akhil was celebrated with great pomp and show. My three brothers and other relatives from India attended this grand occasion.

Rajesh started school at Quarry Hill Infants and was promoted to the Juniors at the age of seven. He completed his junior schooling and gained admission into William Edwards Comprehensive School. He took a keen interest in games and played football and cricket for his school. He also showed great interest in music and passed his O Levels in this subject along with eight other subjects. He went to Palmers Sixth Form College in Grays and passed his A Levels there. He then joined the University of Greenwich. He did his degree in Information Management and got a job in that field. He is now well settled in Reading with his beautiful wife Rita and son Milan.

In 1986, after I was appointed as Senior Psychologist for the South Essex Division, I had two bases – one in Thurrock and the other in Basildon. I now managed two teams of psychologists and other staff. Altogether, there were 31 staff members whom I was directly responsible for. I faced some problems with the Basildon head teachers, who were always critical of psychological services, but I was confident enough to face them with my team of eight psychologists. Each psychologist was responsible for providing efficient service to his or her patch of schools. I would hold weekly meetings where we discussed any issues the team was facing.

There was a good spirit of helping each other. In spite of my increased managerial responsibilities, I kept my own patch of schools and continued with other research projects too. We formulated some training courses for teachers and delivered them all over our area and published the findings in various journals.

In December 1991, I was promoted to the newly created post of Area Educational Psychologist and my salary was upgraded to the next level. In April 1993, the Essex Education Authority awarded me a special performance bonus for my extraordinary performance, which really surprised me. In July 1995, I discussed the issue of my early retirement at the age of 60 with the Principal Psychologist. She was reluctant at first, but agreed when I convinced her that she would save a good deal of money if I retired early. However, she contracted me to work three days a week in four of the Colleges of Further Education in Essex: Thurrock, Basildon, Harlow and South End.

Finally, in July 1995, I bid goodbye to my cherished job. The Director of Education and the Chief Inspector of Schools spoke very highly of my contribution to education in Essex Schools. A number of head teachers came to the retirement party that the staff at the Basildon Education Office held for me. There were real feelings of joy in my heart on this occasion and everyone who came along was brimming with emotion. As I looked back at the years I saw that my rock solid determination had helped me carve out my niche in this country. I was filled with a sense of quiet pride that I had done what I set out to.

7. RETIREMENT WAS JUST THE BEGINNING

After my early retirement, we embarked on a much-awaited, long holiday in India. Pushpa, Bala and I spent a wonderful eight weeks fulfilling our desire to travel to religious and historic sites. This was so different to our other trips, which had been limited to joyous weddings or grief-filled deaths.

This time, we began our holiday in Delhi, from where we went to the much-loved historical town of Agra and saw the Taj Mahal. We then proceeded to Gwalior, Aurangabad, Secunderabad, Hyderabad, Madras, Madurai, Kanya Kumari, Rameshwaram, Bombay, Jaipur, Ajmer and then back to Delhi.

The most wonderful part of the trip was that it gave me the time to pause and reflect. I had just completed a major phase of my life. *What do I want to do now?* This was the question uppermost in my mind.

I had always had a keen interest in giving back to the community. Our three children were well settled and both

Pushpa and I had part-time jobs, so I decided it was the perfect time in my life to volunteer and serve.

My community service began on the 1st of November 1995, when the Thurrock Council appointed me as a governor for two schools – Quarry Hill Infants and Juniors – the schools both of my children had gone to! I was very keen to help the children improve their performance here. I would often put in extra time to support the children, their parents and the teachers in any way possible. I contributed to the school's good governance for a long 19 years, right up until 2013.

As a governor, talking to a group of children at Quarry Hill School

However, this was just part of the opportunity retirement opened up to me. Another deep interest of mine beckoned. In fact, when I followed its call, it opened the door to a whole new life. Retirement turned into rebirth. I had always been interested in politics, so I joined the Labour Party in 1995.

My affiliation to Labour came about because of its humanitarian principles and advocacy of equal opportunity rights. I attended the first ward meeting in October 1995. Thereafter, I was persuaded to attend a day-long training course for the party members where nearly 200 people from different districts attended. I remember, everyone addressed each other as *comrade* to show equality and respect for each other, regardless of colour, religion or sexual orientation. I spent the day eager to learn as much as possible about the Party's policies regarding immigrants. I attended three Party meetings and soon realised that I wanted to stand for Labour Councillor in May 1996, from the Little Thurrock ward.

It was at this point that the first test of integrity presented itself before me. I had to compete with the Sitting Councillor, an ex-Conservative Party member who had resigned six months ago and joined Labour. Most of the older members of the Party did not like him. I happened to meet him right before the selection meeting and he told me that he had been the local Councillor for eight years and was looking forward to contesting the seat once more. After hearing this, I felt it would be morally wrong for me to oust him from his ward, so I withdrew. As you can imagine, this last minute decision of mine did not go down well with those long-standing Labour members who were looking forward to ousting him. But, I was determined to do what was right. The man won, as he was the only candidate left in the fray, and ended up becoming Mayor of the Borough before his retirement from the Council.

I was chosen as the Labour candidate to contest the Council elections from the North Grays ward instead. This was the only ward in the Borough that was a single-member ward and the Conservative Party candidate had usually won it. I thought I was just a paper candidate and that there was no hope for me to win. There were only three Asian families that lived in this ward and they hardly ever voted in the Council elections. I was an outsider, whereas the Tory candidate lived in the ward. Neither my family nor friends thought I could triumph.

However, I began my campaign with confidence and dedication. I made it my mission to contact each and every voter in my ward. The ward was a small one; there were 2500 voters and six weeks to campaign. My election agent, a young enthusiastic girl, wholeheartedly supported me. A number of local Labour Party workers also lent me their hands. My agent and I visited every voter. The positive response from the voters, when I met them, was very encouraging.

The election was held on the 2nd of May 1996 and the results were declared around 11pm the same day. I was elected with 605 votes against the Tory candidate's 318 votes! Imagine my shock and joy! It was a great day for Pushpa and me and we thanked everyone for their great support. I also sent a letter of gratitude to all houses in the ward, assuring them of my commitment to representing their interests in the Council.

A new chapter had started in my life. I was now an elected representative of the people of Thurrock. I remember a few Asian people had stood as Councillors in the past but were never elected, so I became the first Asian Councillor in the history of the Borough. It was a wonderful achievement.

Before the full Council meeting took place, the Chief Executive of the Council met the four newly elected Councillors and arranged a tour of all the departments of the Council for us. It struck me that there were hardly any Asian or Afro-Caribbean officers in the whole Council, with the exception of the Deputy Chief Executive who was of Asian heritage. He was born to Indian parents, but was adopted by a Scottish family while he was still a child. He had been educated in the UK and was married to an English girl. He obviously had no experience of being a newly arrived immigrant from the Asian Subcontinent, but I was pleased to meet him as he showed me warmth.

My first full Council meeting was a truly memorable experience. Everyone was dressed formally in suits. I remember looking around, awe-struck at the Council chamber and the Mayor's high chair. The leader of the Council welcomed the newly elected Councillors as well as the Mayor, who was presiding over the Council meeting. I spoke for just two minutes, quickly thanking everyone for their support.

After that, elections were held for the new Mayor, deputy Mayor and nomination of Councillors for various committees of the Council. I was elected to serve on three committees: Housing, Community Action and Finance. I was also appointed as a member of the management committees of two voluntary organisations: Thurrock CVS (Council of Voluntary Services) and Thurrock CAB (Citizens Advice Bureau).

Later, three sessions were held to explain the roles and responsibilities of a Councillor, and I was also allocated a mentor. I found these sessions very helpful.

I started regular monthly surgery sessions in an old people's complex in my ward. I established a strong relationship with my constituents through this. I also started a monthly newsletter, giving local residents information about my surgery sessions and contact details. I assured them that I would respond to them within 24 hours. I realised that good, honest communication with constituents was the way forward. This strategy proved a great success in winning their confidence throughout my political life.

Soon, a year went by and it was time for elections again. How time had passed! I had settled into my new role as a Councillor and was in fact thoroughly enjoying it.

As I mentioned earlier, my ward, Grays North, was a single-member ward, and until my election had always been a Tory stronghold. The Party wanted to strengthen Labour's

Visiting an old people's home as a Councillor

influence in the area and recommended merging it with adjoining areas and creating a new, three-member ward called Grays Thurrock. The boundary commission accepted this suggestion.

On the 1st of May 1997, both the borough and parliamentary elections took place in the country. Labour won both. I won my seat along with two other Labour candidates from the newly formed Grays Thurrock Ward.

At the full Council meeting, I was elected to serve as the vice chair of two committees: Community Action and Pride in Thurrock Working Panel. I worked hard on both of these and it brought me in touch with a large number of local organisations and residents.

As a Councillor my main duty was to identify the needs of residents in my ward and to raise these at every level in the Council. The main concerns of the people in my ward were to improve the state of the roads, the cleanliness of pathways and road safety. In particular, we needed to improve traffic congestion near the five schools in the ward. We improved things steadily with the help of the Council officers and the residents, until cuts started to affect these services in later years.

There were two other important areas that needed my attention: to start building bridges between the Council and the local BAME communities and to promote volunteer work inside and outside the Council. I started turning my attention to these too.

My hard work paid off and the people of my ward elected me in all seven elections that I fought during my twenty years' service as a local Councillor.

8. MAKING THE WORLD A BETTER PLACE

I can never forget my initial years in England as a newly arrived migrant. No wonder then, that empowering migrant communities was a significant part of my political agenda. I wanted to see and contribute to a truly integrated and mutually respectful society.

Soon after I became a Councillor, I was invited to attend a meeting of black, Asian and ethnic minority (BAME) Councillors from all over the country at the House of Commons by a prominent Asian Member of Parliament, Hon. Keith Vaz. It was so wonderful to meet other Asian Councillors. We shared our similar experiences with each other: establishing ourselves politically and winning the confidence of the majority white voters. I became a member of this National Association of BAME Councillors. The next year, I was elected into its management committee, where I stayed for a number of years 'til 2008. I left when infighting began. I was simply not interested in factional politics.

I also started focusing on ways to empower the BAME community and set up a group towards this. After eighteen months of work, the group recommended establishing a voluntary community organisation, which would work with other organisations to help to strengthen the local BAME communities and improve their access to services.

An application for a grant of £280,000 was submitted to the Home Office. The application was accepted and the TRUST (Thurrock Racial Unity Task Group) came into operation as an independent voluntary charitable organisation in July 2000. This organisation has done a great job of representing the interests of the BAME communities.

While I was busy in setting up the TRUST, I was also working with a group of Asian elders to set up the Thurrock Asian Association, a voluntary community charitable organisation, which would strengthen the local Asian community.

This Association came about because of a very sad incident that I witnessed. I was walking to the Council office and passed through the town centre. To my horror, I saw four Asian older people sitting on a bench and three young white teenagers spitting and swearing at them. There were a few people standing around, watching this ugly scene. It left me extremely disturbed. I arrived at the Council and immediately went and met the manager of the Community Action team and asked her to ring the police and take action against these youngsters. I also asked for her advice about finding a suitable safe place for these Asian elders to spend their time.

The Asian community had been living in Thurrock since the 1950s. These were mainly people from the rural areas of Punjab who came here to earn money and build better lives for their children. They were uneducated but hardworking people, who worked in the local cement and other factories. They did not interact with the local community and hardly ever took advantage of any facilities and benefits provided by the Council. They kept themselves to themselves and their lives revolved around the Sikh temple in Grays. I wanted a safe haven for them where they could develop their confidence and build bridges with the local community.

I had my first meeting with five local Asian residents in my home, where I put forward my idea of a voluntary organisation that would campaign for a local community Asian Centre. We had another meeting at the Sikh temple, where nearly 80 local Asian residents turned up.

The Thurrock Asian Association was thus born on the 12th of September 1999. We elected and put in place a management committee. I was elected President unanimously. We drew up a constitution and got charitable status. In 2001, we were able to hire an old dilapidated shop from the Council, which we transformed into The Thurrock Asian Resource Centre, Clarence Road, Grays. Slowly but surely our dream came to life.

This centre has been widely used by various age groups for activities such as singing, dancing, health programmes like yoga and tai chi, English classes, social get-togethers, festival celebrations and meetings for elders. It was heart-warming to see the Asian community open up, connect and bloom.

The Asian Association's first Diwali celebrations, with the music group in 1999

Thurrock Asian Association celebrating Holi with the Mayor

Celebrating Dashant with the local Nepalese community

At the same time, my children's lives were flowering too! It is a parent's dream to see his child marry and settle down. So, it was a blessed day when Raj's marriage was fixed with Rita. Raj and Rita got married in grand style on the 27th of September 1998 at the Civic Hall Grays, in the presence of 300 guests. They settled down and set up home in Reading, Berkshire.

I continued my part-time job as a psychologist and Pushpa continued working part-time at the ASDA store in Tilbury.

In terms of my work as a Councillor, I also promoted the cause of equal opportunities within the Council as much as

Raj and Rita's wedding

outside it. The Council set up a Diversity Department headed by a well-qualified manager who worked hard to train the Council staff in promoting equality in all their work.

I wanted to put my energy into supporting not just the BAME community, but the other most vulnerable members of society as well. I think the strength of a society lies in how it takes care of its weakest – the elders, the children, the minorities and the sick. I had observed that the people of the Borough had always had problems accessing good primary health care services and I wanted to change that. I got the opportunity to do so when I was appointed the Non-Executive Director on the board of the Thurrock Primary Care Trust.

One of the issues in accessing medical care in the Borough was a shortage of general practitioners. We recruited a number of Spanish doctors to amend this, but sadly they went back after two to three years and we were left in the same situation all over again. However, I did have some success. I appointed an additional chiropodist to expand the medical resources of the Borough. There were also five older people's complexes in my ward, with two hundred residents. I started attending a regular monthly meeting with the residents and the housing manager. The residents would talk about their problems and we would improve facilities for their daily living on the basis of their feedback.

I fought my third election as a Councillor on 6th May 1999 and secured 821 votes against 343 for the Conservative and 119 for the Liberal Democrat candidates.

Because of the Council's new unitary Status, for which I had worked, the new governing constitution of Cabinet and Scrutiny Committees came into operation. I was selected to serve on the Scrutiny Committee of the Council and in the next four years I chaired four Scrutiny Panels, which produced four reports on important issues faced by the residents of the Borough.

The first Scrutiny Panel investigated the state of overgrown grass on the footpaths of the Borough. A number of local residents had complained about this issue. After a thorough investigation, the panel made eighteen recommendations for improving the grass cutting services, which were approved by the Cabinet.

The second Scrutiny Panel that I chaired looked at the local bus services in the Borough. A number of elderly residents had complained about the poor bus services in the Borough. A thorough investigation was carried out and the report was compiled in April 2001 with 35 recommendations for improving the bus services in the Borough. This report and its recommendations were widely circulated and supported by the local press. This resulted in improvements.

Over the next two years, I was elected chairman of the Children's Education Panel and we produced two very important scrutiny reports on education. The first was, "Report of a Review into Education Standards at Thurrock Schools." And the second was, "A Review of Policy on Special Educational Needs Provision in Thurrock." The recommendations of these reports were sent to all local schools and also to the Department of Education and Sciences. These reports were published in 2002 and 2003 and were well received by the local schools.

In the middle of all the hard work came a very sweet prize. Pushpa and I were invited to the Queen's Garden Party at Buckingham Palace with the Mayor and Mayoress of Thurrock! It was a dream come true.

During all our years of living in England, we had often joined the visitors thronging at the gates of Buckingham Palace. We had stood at the magnificent gates and watched the ceremonious changing of the guards, all the while hoping to catch a glimpse of royalty. But the 18th of July 2001 was different.

On that day, we went beyond those gates. We drove into the palace in a chauffeur-driven car. Pushpa wore her best sari and I wore my best three-piece suit. The garden was huge and next to a lake. There were two big canopies in the garden, one was for VVIPs, including the Queen, and the other was for everyone else. People queued up for the scrumptious cakes, biscuits, sandwiches, tea and coffee. We walked around the garden leisurely as we waited for the Queen to make her appearance.

When the Queen and the Duke arrived, we formed two lines to receive them. She would occasionally stop and chat with some lucky person. The Royal Family assembled on a raised platform and we could see them well as we were only a few yards away.

After we finished at the palace, we went to the House of Commons, another new experience. We were welcomed there by two Members of Parliament and we had dinner with them in the Members Canteen. They showed us around the Palace of Westminster and we saw the Chamber where MPs debate. We also had a peek at the House of Lords. After this visit to the Buckingham Palace, we were lucky to have two more – in 2006 and 2013, which I will describe later in this chapter.

My fourth Council election took place on the 2nd of May 2002, which I won again with a good majority. I was hoping to become a Cabinet Member but internal party politics ruined my chances. There were three factions and each one was pushing their candidate forward. I, on the other hand, did not belong to any group. Power struggles are dirty and I did not want any part of it.

At the Annual General Meeting of the Labour Group in May 2003, the group decided that along with the election of the Leader and Deputy Leader, we should also elect Cabinet Members. This decision proved advantageous to me, as I was one of the seven Councillors who were elected to become Cabinet Members. The leader offered me the portfolio of Cabinet Member for Highways, Transport and Europe. During my one year as a Cabinet Member, I achieved two important things: Firstly I was able to introduce a free bus pass for older people of the Borough a year before the central government introduced it in 2004. Secondly, I started the process of twinning Thurrock Council with Plock Council in Poland.

I had now established myself as an adept Councillor in the Borough. I was also known outside of it for my work with the National Association of BAME Councillors.

To become even more effective on the national scene, I became an Accredited Peer with the Improvement & Development Agency (IDeA), a part of the Local Government Association. As an Accredited Peer, I was a part of peer review teams that helped Councils in improving their services to local residents. From 2003 to 2012 I visited twenty Councils all over the country as a part of peer review teams and helped them to improve their services to residents.

A visit to Japan brought home to me how grace-filled my life was. The Japan Local Government Centre in London had been organising tours for Councillors and officers from the UK to Japan to strengthen bonds between the local authorities of both countries. I too had the opportunity to go, from the 5th to the 16th October 2003.

As I sat on the top floor of the five-star hotel we were staying at in Tokyo, sipping fine brandy and gazing the beautiful cityscape through a big window, I remember vividly thinking: *how is it possible that a village boy from India is sitting on the tenth floor of a five star hotel in Tokyo and enjoying the beauty of the night in this great city?* Convinced that it was God's Grace, I knelt down on the floor and thanked the Almighty. I shared

With a Japanese family in Tokyo, 2003

this incident with my elder brother when I went to India and he remarked that this good luck was because of the blessings of our dearest mum.

I really enjoyed Japan and I produced a detailed report about the lessons I learnt on our tour of three local authorities.

In 2003, I was selected to serve as one of the directors on the board of the Thurrock Development Corporation, which was started by the central government to expedite the regeneration of the Borough of Thurrock. For me, this was a great honour and opportunity to serve the local people.

With colleagues on our tour of Japan

In May 2004, the Labour Party lost 17 Council seats to the Conservative party. However in the Grays Thurrock ward I won my seat with a good majority and my two other Labour colleagues also won their seats with reduced majorities.

The Conservatives formed the administration. The immediate effect was that I lost my position as a Cabinet Member. However, I continued working as a Shadow Cabinet Member of Highways and Transport.

In 2005, the Labour Party won the parliamentary elections under the leadership of Prime Minister Tony Blair. The mood was jubilant and I attended the Annual National Labour Party

Conference. I had the opportunity to meet the top leadership of the Labour Party including the Prime Minister, the Home Minister, the Chancellor of the Exchequer, the Foreign Secretary and a host of other ministers. Interestingly, there were no special guards to protect them. This really surprised me, as my experience of Indian political leaders was that they were always surrounded by a large number of security people at any public meeting.

The main objective of this conference was to find consensus on the Party's policies on important political issues. When it came to issues like the building of more Council houses, I clapped enthusiastically to show my approval.

Something else happened in 2005 that made me feel that I had built my reputation as an efficient and effective Councillor both within the Council and with my constituents.

I received a letter on the 18th of November 2005 that left me absolutely shocked. It was a letter from the Prime Minister's office. My eyes could hardly take it in. The Prime Minister wrote that he was recommending my name for the Queen's Honours List. I read it three times, just to make sure and then shouted out with joy!

The list came out on the 31st of December and I was on it. I was going to receive the Member of the Most Excellent Order of the British Empire (MBE) Award! The Council's Communication Officer was the first to spot my name in *the Daily Telegraph* and congratulate me. The number of congratulatory messages, cards and emails overwhelmed me.

Elizabeth the Second, *by the Grace of God of the United Kingdom of Great Britain and Northern Ireland and of Her other Realms and Territories Queen, Head of the Commonwealth, Defender of the Faith and Sovereign of the Most Excellent Order of the British Empire to Our trusty and well beloved Yash Pall Gupta Esquire*

Greeting

Whereas *We have thought fit to nominate and appoint you to be an Ordinary Member of the Civil Division of Our said Most Excellent Order of the British Empire*

We do *by these presents grant unto you the Dignity of an Ordinary Member of Our said Order and hereby authorise you to have hold and enjoy the said Dignity and Rank of an Ordinary Member of Our aforesaid Order together with all and singular the privileges thereunto belonging or appertaining.*

Given *at Our Court at Saint James's under Our Sign Manual and the Seal of Our said Order this Thirty-first day of December 2005 in the Fifty-fourth year of Our Reign.*

By the Sovereign's Command.

Grand Master.

Grant of the Dignity of an Ordinary Member of the Civil Division of the Order of the British Empire to Councillor Yash Pall Gupta

Thus, the New Year of 2006 started on a great note – news of the MBE award and wait, even more good news – my daughter-in-law was pregnant! I was going to be a grandfather once more.

I was now eagerly waiting for the day I would receive the award from the Queen at Buckingham Palace. It arrived on the 15th of February, 2006. What a memorable day it was! We drove into Buckingham Palace, with Pushpa, Raj and our grandson in the Mayor's chauffeur-driven car. Everyone was dressed up for this big occasion.

The chauffeur-driven Mayor's car

There were 96 recipients of the Honour Awards and 250 guests. At 10:50am, we were lined up and led towards the Grand Hall where we were going to be presented with our awards. The Queen entered the Hall with her Gurkha Body Guards at 11am. The strains of the National Anthem flooded the Hall, after which the awardees were presented to the Queen, one by one. I was quite nervous when I heard my name, but also felt thrilled. I bowed and when I raised my head, she attached a medal to my coat. We chatted very briefly, after which she shook my hands and congratulated me. I stepped back and an officer took my medal and put it into a case.

The Queen left after the ceremony and I re-joined Pushpa, Raj and Ravi. A professional photographer met us outside the doors of the Palace and took pictures. I also ordered a video of this memorable event for everyone in our family to view. The local Sikh temple invited me to their Sunday gathering and honoured me with a Saropa. I really felt humbled and thanked everyone for this honour.

Shaking hands with the Queen for my MBE Award, February 2006

With Raj, Pushpa and Ravi at Buckingham Palace after receiving my MBE Award

Being honoured with a Saropa at the Sikh temple after receiving my MBE

Later in that blessed year, our lovely grandson Milan was born on the 7th of September. What more could I ask for? Such a sweet, lovely and smart baby! God bless him with a happy long life.

Towards the end of the year, we went to India for a family wedding. An important outcome of our visit was the establishment of the Gupta Charitable Trust, a registered charity. The purpose of this Trust was to provide financial help to ten bright, aspiring young children from poor families for their further education. Each pupil would get a grant of

Giving out scholarships to students with my brothers, India, 2011

Rs. 10,000. The students were to be selected by a panel of judges made up of local teachers and my brothers.

40 young boys and girls were helped by these grants from secondary schools in Dhariwal, the town where my family settled down after Indian Independence. However, there were problems in the selection process in the coming years and my brothers decided to suspend the grants.

In October 2014, I went to India and had a meeting with the teachers to evaluate the work of the charity. They assured us that the grants were most definitely supporting the further education of these students. The head teachers agreed to nominate ten deserving candidates each year. We decided to evaluate the impact of these grants after a period of three years.

I continued to be busy with public life and working as a Shadow Cabinet Member for Communities and Environment. I performed my scrutiny role by asking my counterpart Cabinet Member relevant questions. The monthly surgeries for residents in my area continued, as did the monthly reports about my work as a Councillor that went on to the Council's web page for residents' information.

I maintained my voluntary work with seven organisations by serving on their management committees. The organisations where I worked as a volunteer Trustee were: Thurrock CVS, Thurrock Open Door, Thurrock Racial Unity Task Group, Thurrock Faith Matters, Thurrock Citizens Advice Bureau, Thurrock Community Chest and of course the Thurrock Asian Association.

On the 2nd of May 2008, I fought my sixth Council election and won it with 1011 votes.

Just a few days after, I received an email from the Indian International Friendship Society based in Delhi, India informing me that I had been nominated for the 'Glory of India' Award for my services in promoting friendship between India and the United Kingdom. I was invited to receive this award at a ceremony at the Radisson Hotel in London on the 28th of June, 2008. I was thrilled to learn that many prominent Indians such as Mother Teresa of Calcutta had received this

GLORY OF INDIA AWARD
Presented to Cllr Yash Gupta M.B.E. on Saturday 28th June, 2008 at the Radison Hotel—London

l-r Cllr Yash Gupta, Dr Bishma N Singh, (Former Governor), Virendra Sharma M.P., Marsha Singh M.P. Lord Sheik

Receiving the Glory of India Award at the Radisson Hotel in London, 28th of June 2008

renowned award previously. There were more than 200 people who came from all over the world for the award ceremony. I received my award from the Honourable Minister of the Indian High Commission. I met some prominent members of the Asian community there such as our three members of Parliament and High Court Judge, Honourable Mota Singh.

In January 2010, the Leader of the Labour Group also nominated me for a national award for Community Champion Councillor of the Year, being organised by the Local Government Information Unit (LGIU). This award was open to all 24,000 Councillors in the country.

GLORY OF INDIA AWARD

Presented to

CLLR YASH GUPTA M.B.E

For Outstanding Achievements & Distinguished Globol Services

by

Hon'ble Shri. Madhava Chandra

Minister High Commission of India (U.K.)
At the 28th International Congress of NRIs
on Saturday, 28th June, 2008 at London

Gurpreet Singh
Secretary General

Organised by :
INDIA INTERNATIONAL FRIENDSHIP SOCIETY

On the 4th of February 2010, I received this award at the famous Emirate Stadium in London from Cllr. Wilcox, President of the LGUI. This award was well publicised in the press. At the full Council meeting the Mayor congratulated me for putting Thurrock Council on the national map. I was also on the front page of magazine *Cllr* with the words, "Meet the Councillor Community Champion", and there was two pages of coverage of my work.

On the 6th of May 2010, there were parliamentary and Council elections. The Labour Party lost the election. At the local level, it was a hung Council. At the annual Council meeting, the Labour Group nominated me as the Deputy

Receiving the Community Champion Councillor of the Year Award from Cllr. David Wilcox

Mayor for the Borough, but I lost against the Tory candidate by one vote.

However, the Labour Party and a few independent Councillors formed the administration for the first time since 2004. I was appointed the Cabinet Member for Environmental Services including Highways and Transport. It was a big portfolio, which dealt with many local services, and I worked hard to provide efficient services.

After the May 2011 Council elections, Thurrock was still a hung Council. On the 25th of May 2011, I was elected the Deputy Mayor by a majority of 2 votes at the Full Council meeting. I felt my dream of becoming the first Asian Mayor of the Borough was nearing fulfilment.

The truth is that I could have become Mayor in 2011 itself. However, racial prejudice got in the way. The Labour Group had decided to nominate me as Mayor because of my seniority and my colleague, Cllr. Curtis as the Deputy Mayor. The Tory Group decided to put forward their previous Deputy Mayor as their candidate for the Mayor. The election of the Mayor depended on the *single* vote of the outgoing Mayor, as it was a hung Council.

Two days before the election, the Labour Leadership met the outgoing Mayor and shared Cllr. Curtis's and my name with her. She also knew that her Deputy Mayor, Cllr. Ojetola, a black Councillor, was the Tory nominee for the post of the Mayor. She categorically refused to support Cllr. Ojetola's or my nomination for the post of Mayor. She was, however, willing to support Cllr. Curtis, if his name was put forward for the job, as he was white.

The Leader of the Labour Group spoke to me about this critical situation. After a lot of thinking, I decided to do the one thing that I had not done before – to accept racial discrimination in the wider interest of the Party and Borough. I asked them to put forward Cllr. Curtis's name as Mayor and mine as Deputy.

Since I became Councillor, I had experienced various incidents of racial prejudice from other Councillors and officers, but was able to tackle them in a civilised way. Over the

c'llr.

INFORMATION AND INSPIRATION FOR COUNCILLORS
FROM THE LOCAL GOVERNMENT INFORMATION UNIT

MY PATCH
MEETS THE C'LLR
COMMUNITY CHAMPION

DENHAM AND
SPELMAN ON
LOCALISM

COUNCILLORS
AND SOCIAL
MEDIA

LGiU

years, I've learnt that you can't change behaviour by creating conflict, but by setting a good example of your own.

I started my job as the Deputy Mayor of the Borough and attended nearly 60 events inside and outside the Borough on behalf on the Mayor. This was good preparation for my role as Mayor.

9. THE FINAL DESTINATION

The year 2012 was remarkably significant. Three very important events occurred in my life.

I celebrated my golden wedding anniversary on the 9th of March. I won my seventh and final Council election on the 3rd of May and I was unanimously elected as Mayor of the Borough on the 23rd of May.

Pushpa and I completed 50 years of married life together; these were years in which we supported each other and brought up our three children and lovely grandchildren. We had our ups and downs but persevered and set a good example for our family.

We spent the day with our beautiful family. They first took us to the famous Bhakti Vedant Temple at Watford, early in the morning, where we prayed and thanked the Almighty for our long and happy married life and sought His blessings for the coming years. The children then took us to watch a comedy film at a cinema house in London and then to a posh dinner at a restaurant.

We celebrated with relatives and friends at the New Delhi restaurant in Grays High Street on the 11th of March. Music and dancing enlivened the air. Good food satisfied our taste buds. Nearly 70 guests enjoyed the day with us. What a lovely time we had!

Two months later, I stood for my seventh and final Council election. I won this election with a majority of 748 votes – the highest amongst all seventeen Councillors elected. The election result for the Grays Thurrock ward was: Yash Gupta – Labour 1073, Conservative 325, UKIP 242 and the Lib.

Me and my wife, Mayor and
Mayoress of Thurrock

Pushpa and I celebrating our
Golden Wedding Anniversary

Dem. 82. I sent a personal letter of thanks to all the voters in my ward in which I wrote: *It's a tremendous honour to be re-elected to serve as your Councillor. Your continued support really means a great deal to me.*

The day I had been waiting for had finally arrived. I was elected as Mayor of the Borough on the 23rd of May 2012, at the Annual General Meeting of the Council. At last, my life's greatest wish had come to fruition! I had come to this country as a migrant many, many years ago and here I was now, its First Citizen.

Campaigning for election as
Labour Councillor, 2012   *Dressed in my Mayoral outfit*

I was the first Asian Mayor of the Borough of Thurrock since it was established in 1974. I conveyed my thanks to all those people in the Council and in the community who had made it possible for me to achieve this very honourable position. I would now chair the full Council meetings and represent Her Majesty, the Queen, at social and cultural events within the Borough and outside.

After my election as Mayor, I made three announcements:

1. I chose Pushpa, my wife, as the Mayoress.
2. I selected the Thurrock Community Chest as the Mayor's Charity of the Year.
3. I also declared Rev. Darren Barlow, a local priest and a friend, as Mayor's Chaplain.

Cllr. Tony Fish, a long-standing Councillor, became the Deputy Mayor with me. My mayoral engagements started the very next day.

with Reverend Darren Barlow, Parmers
College, Grays

Mayor Yash Gupta and
Deputy Mayor Tony Fish

It was a very busy but enjoyable year of my life. I attended 375 events, which was a record in itself! There were some memorable events, which I would like to mention here:

On the 30th of May 2012, I welcomed the Duke of Kent who paid a visit to the Royal Opera House Production Park.

On the 2nd of June 2012, I inaugurated the famous Community Cultural Thurrock Festival, which attracted nearly 10,000 visitors over a two-day period.

Chairing a Council meeting

I attended a few events organised by various local organisations to celebrate the Queen's Jubilee on the 3rd, 4th and 5th of June, 2012.

As the Mayor of the Borough, I attended at least twelve citizenship ceremonies at the registrar's office, where I handed over the Citizenship Certificate to those people who had come from various other countries and made the UK their home. I was always happy to share my experiences with them and encouraged them to integrate with the local communities through voluntary work.

Celebrating the Queen's Jubilee with the local residents

Because of my interest in children's education, I also visited a number of local schools during the year. I invited eight schools to send a few children to visit the Council and meet with me in the Mayor's Parlour. I wanted children to develop a relationship with their Council. On my request, a special initiative was launched. Teachers were asked to nominate two high-achieving children for the Mayor's Award. As many as twenty young boys and girls attended this event with their teachers and parents and were awarded certificates. This event was organised to raise the educational aspirations of the young boys and girls in our schools.

A very sweet part of my duties was to attend two 100th birthday celebrations of two ladies who were living in local care homes in the Borough! As a Councillor, I always championed the cause of older people and visited at least twenty older peoples' complexes during my term.

In July 2012, I led the World Olympic Torch Relay parade through Grays town centre, which was cheered by thousands of residents.

In October 2012, I attended three main community events: Black History Month, Asian Diwali Festival and

A celebration of young people's achievements

Dasain celebrations by the local Gurkha Community. These celebrations helped cement inter-community relationships.

In December there were Christmas party invitations from a number of Mayors of the different districts in Essex. I must have attended fifteen such parties and obviously put on at least a few pounds after that!

The New Year was dedicated to remembering sombrely, as the 31st of January 2013 marked the 60th anniversary of the tragic floods that had snatched away many lives in Essex,

Welcoming the Olympic Torch as Mayor

Visiting Poland with other Mayors and Mayoresses, 2012

Belgium and the Netherlands. It was commemorated at the Chelmsford Cathedral and a number of Mayors, including myself, attended. Princess Diana also attended this function , along with survivors of those floods and the local people.

In February and March 2013, I was busy attending civic dinners organised by various mayors of different boroughs and districts. On the 19th of April 2013, the Thurrock Mayor's Civic Dinner was organised by the Council.

This was the big event of my Mayoral year. Pushpa and I were the chief hosts. 260 guests attended this event at the Civic Hall, Grays, including the Lord Lieutenant, High Sherriff of

Remembrance Day with Lord Lieutenant Peter

Essex, Members of Parliament, fifteen mayors, Councillors, local dignitaries, Council officers and the representatives of various Thurrock communities and businesses. Fourteen members of my family were also present.

The hall was decorated smartly and visitors were welcomed with a glass of champagne. I greeted everyone and gave a short speech outlining some important aspects of my work as the Mayor of Thurrock. The Leader of the Council proposed a toast to my very successful mayoral year. A five-course meal and Bhangra music and dancing followed. Everyone enjoyed themselves thoroughly!

The celebration of the Mayor's Civic Dinner

At the Annual General Meeting of the Council on the 22nd of May 2013, I handed over the Mayoral position to Cllr. Tony Fish and expressed my gratitude to everyone present. The Leader of the Council and the Opposition Leader commended my work as the Mayor of the Borough.

What a fantastic, enjoyable and memorable year of my life! The final Mayoral engagement of the year was fittingly a visit to the Queen's Garden Party on the 30th of May 2013.

The Queen's Garden Party, May 2013

By Appointment to
Her Majesty The Queen
Supplier of Audio Visual Services
British Ceremonial Arts Limited
Wokingham

Buckingham Palace
Summer Garden Parties

During the year I attended as many as 375 events, received 45 letters of appreciation and raised funds for my charity, The Thurrock Community Chest. The local press paid warm tributes to my work.

After my Mayoral year, I felt really tired and the old age seemed to have crept up on me. I had some problems with my right leg, which affected my brisk walking. I decided to slow down and reduce the number of hours I spent working for the Council and community. This time, I didn't ask for a Cabinet role, but did accept the responsibility of Chair of the Health and Well Being Scrutiny Committee. I worked very hard to improve local health and social services.

I was also asked by the Leader of the Council to attend the Annual Conference of Local Government Association on his behalf. It was my first time attending such an important meeting regarding Local Government. It was a massive event, like a Mela. I got to meet the leadership of the Local Government Association and discuss pertinent local issues like the cut in the central government's grants to the local authorities and its impact on the delivery of services. In spite of this criticism, the Secretary of State warned us to expect more cuts in the next few years.

The year went by and I continued my work in the Council as well as in the local community. I was selected to chair the Corporate Overview and Scrutiny Committee; I also became a member of the SACRE, Health and well-being Scrutiny Committee and Standards and Audit Committee. I continued doing my best to fulfil my role in these committees and also in the community. However, I was feeling the effect of old age as my senses and body parts were getting weaker.

I had the desire to make a final visit to India to meet my sisters, brothers and their families. Pushpa did not want to go as she felt that there would be care issues with Bala. So, I went in September 2014 and enjoyed the company of my extended family. I must say I got VVIP treatment from my family! I also met the head teachers of four schools in my hometown and discussed restarting the grants for deserving students.

With the dawn of 2015, I decided to reduce my active role in the Council as well as in the voluntary sector. I resigned from my position as trustee from the Thurrock CAB as well as Thurrock Racial Unity Task Group. I had served these organisations for nearly eighteen years and did my best to develop their services. Unfortunately, these organisations were now riddled with financial problems because of cuts in grants.

The 2015 Council elections resulted in a hung Council between Labour, UKIP and the Conservative parties. At the Annual General Meeting of the Council, the Labour Group kept control of the Council with the support of UKIP. The chairs and the vice chairs of the Scrutiny Panels were divided between the three parties. I was elected as the Vice Chair of the Children's Scrutiny Committee and also kept my membership to various other committees and voluntary organisations. I was also nominated to represent the Council on the Thurrock

Arts Council. I was already serving as a Board Member of the Advisory Board of the Thameside Children's Centre.

These duties kept me quite busy, but it was time to take a break and relax as I approached my 80th birthday. There was also an event that I was very proud to attend after my birthday on the 23rd of July, 2015. It was the day my granddaughter Seema (Renu's younger child) graduated from the School of Oriental and African Studies, University of London. She is a very intelligent, hard-working, sweet girl and I am so happy about her achievements. Renu's first-born, Ravi, studied at the London School of Economics. We attended his graduation ceremony too, two years earlier on the 18th of June, 2013. He is a very bright, smart-looking young man who is now completing his course as a Chartered Accountant.

My immediate family celebrated my birthday on the 5th of July by invoking blessings with a religious ceremony conducted by a renowned Hindu Priest at home.

On the 19th of July 2015, we had a grand celebratory event with family and friends at the Orsett Hall Hotel. We celebrated my 80th birthday with food, drinks and music. My son and three grandchildren said some truly wonderful things about me and others praised my work in the Council and the local communities generously.

The local press wrote about me on occasion – the editor of YourThurrock.com, *The Thurrock Gazette*, *The Thurrock Enquirer* and *The Speak Out*, the monthly journal of the Thurrock CVS, to name a few.

Seema's Graduation   *Ravi's Graduation*

The chief reporter of the *Thurrock Gazette* wrote: *Speaking with Mr Gupta, you could see why he has been elected seven times as a councillor over the last 19 years. He is a man you believe when he speaks to you and he cares deeply about the community here in Thurrock and breaking down barriers, whether racial or health. His work in helping to set up Thurrock Mind many years ago is testament to that. Mr Gupta is a model councillor and a model politician. Whatever your political persuasion, there can be no denying the important role he has played in Thurrock over the years. Some in the chamber could learn a lot from him before he*

Celebrating my 80th birthday with my whole family

retires next year. *So happy birthday Yash, and enjoy your 20th and final year.*

The headlines in the *Thurrock Enquirer* said: *Cllr Yash Gupta MBE, former Mayor of Thurrock, Champion Councillor and a great family man celebrating his 80th birthday.*

The editor of YourThurrock.com wrote on my 80th Birthday: *Cllr Gupta has been a considerable force in the council chamber for the last nineteen years but that was just after he retired as a senior psychologist. Yash Gupta has lived a remarkable life and is (in our opinion) the embodiment of dignity, civic pride and aspiration.*

With my classmate and close friend Duggal

I have told everyone that I will be retiring from my public life in May 2016 after completing my term as a Councillor. I will also reduce my commitment to my voluntary work. I hope to spend the rest of my life caring for my wife, my daughter Bala and myself.

Bala attends the day care centre in Grays. She also receives direct payments and gets twenty hours a week care help from the social services. She is getting old and is now 52 years old. Her main problems are that she is hard of hearing, has very little verbal communication, poor understanding and is dependent on us for her daily living. Pushpa has been looking after her

celebrating Milan's first birthday, with Rita, Raj, Milan and Pushpa

and teaches her to be as independent as she can. Sometimes I help her as well, but she listens to Pushpa more than she does to me. Bala is a very happy young lady who is very content and does not make any demands. She likes helping others in her own limited way. She is living happily with us at home and is very attached to her mum. Both of them are emotionally close and find it a great strain to be separated from each other. I would like to make some permanent arrangement for her future living as soon as possible but Pushpa does not want me to talk about it at present.

My search for Soul will take priority for the rest of my life. The next book I hope to write will be about my spiritual experiences.

Pushpa and me have been married for over 53 years and she has been a great support to me in my life. She is a very good cook and prepares delicious food every day, which I eat with great delight. She has worked extremely hard all her life, especially in the days when we came here with no money at all. She looked after the children when I went to Swansea for a year. I could not have accomplished so much in my life without her. She backed me during my Council elections, though sometimes very grudgingly. But I will say this, she is a good wife and a caring partner and I can't thank her enough for her help and support in my life.

Me and Pushpa, the elected Mayor and Mayoress of Thurrock, 2013

this
ILLUMINATED
DIPLOMA ❖

announces and celebrates the achievements of the
individual undersigned

Cllr. Yash Gupta M.B.E.

DICTIONARY OF
INTERNATIONAL
BIOGRAPHY

37th Edition

Signed & Sealed at the International Biographical Centre,
CAMBRIDGE, ENGLAND.

April 2013

Date

Editor in Chief

A LIST OF RESEARCH ARTICLES PUBLISHED BY
MR. YASH P. GUPTA, M.A. M.Ed. Dip.Ed.PSYCH.
SENIOR EDUCATIONAL PSYCHOLOGIST, SOUTH WEST ESSEX

1. "A Psychologist with a Withdrawal Group in Thurrock"
    Essex Education (1977) Vol. 31, No.3

2. "The Educational and Vocational Aspirations of Asian Immigrant and English School Leavers.
    A Comparative Study"
    The British Journal of Sociology (1977) Vol. XXVIII, 2, pp 185-198

3. "Behavioural Problems in an EPS School in Essex"
    Therapeutic Education (1978) Vol. 6, No.2, pp 12-20

4. "Some Observations after two years of Group Work with Teachers in Thurrock"
    Therapeutic Education (1980) Vol. 8, No.2, pp 16-22

5. "The Roles of the Educational Psychologist as seen by a Group of Psychologists and a Group of
    Headteachers"
    Links (1980) Vol. 6, No.1, pp 17-21

6. "Identification of Infant Children with Poor Learning Skills"
    Remedial Education (1981) Vol. 16, No.3, pp 137-142

7. "Some Problems in the Identification of the Intellectually Bright Infant Children"
    Links (1980) Vol. 5, No.2, pp 22-28

8. "Support Group for Thurrock Secondary School Teachers"
    Essex Education (1982) Vol. 35, No.2

9. "The Children with Epileptic Fits: Some Facts and Observations"
    Links (1985) Vol. 10, No.2, pp 12-15

10. "The Gifted Children in our Schools - Their Identification and Education"
    Links (1985) Vol. 10, No.3, pp 9-14

11. "Headteachers Too Need Pastoral Support"
    Educational Psychology in Practice (1985) Vol. 1, No.3

12. "Group Counselling Sessions at a Comprehensive School in Thurrock"
    by Y. Gupta and J. Ayres
    Essex Education (1985) Autumn 1985, pp 5-8

13. "Teaching Spelling"
    by S. Bayley, Y. Gupta and J. Bold
    Perspectives (1985) Vol. 1, No.5, pp 8-11

Cont/d......

14. "Stress on Adolescents"
    Perspectives (1985) Vol. 1, No.4

15. "Behaviour Modification and the Classroom Teacher: A Positive Approach to Classroom Management"
    Links (1986) Vol. 11, No.2

16. "Some Observations on the Work of a Tutorial Unit in Thurrock"
    The Journal of Special Education (1986) Vol. 13, No.3

17. "Three Different Modes of Parental Involvement in their Children's Reading"
    Links (1987) Vol. 12, No.2, pp 12-17

18. "Educational Psychologists and Racial Issues: Some Observations"
    AEP Circulation (1987)

19. "Portage Home Teaching Project in Thurrock - Some Observations"
    Links (1988) Vol. 13, No.2

20. "Attending and Chairing Meetings - Some Suggestions for Improvements"
    Essex Education, Winter 1988/89

21. "Attending Meetings: Chairing Meetings - Some Suggestions for Improvements"
    Links (1989) Vol. 14, No.2, pp 17-20

22. "A Case Study of an Elective Mute"
    Links (Summer 1990) Vol. 15, No.3, pp 5-8

23. "A Study in the Improvement of School Attendance in a Comprehensive School"
    Links (Autumn 1990) Vol. 16, No.1, pp 11-16

24. "Talking with Parents of Dyslexic Children: The Value of Skilled Discussion Methods"
    J. Acklaw and Y. Gupta
    Support for Learning Vol. 6, No.1 (1991)

25. J. Acklaw and Y. Gupta (1991)
    "Talking with Parents of Dyslexic Children"
    in M. Hinson (Ed.)
    "Teachers and Special Education Needs: Coping with Change"
    London: Longman

26. "Management of Lunchtime Behaviour - A Course for Mid-day Assistants"
    (1995) Underprint

Cont/d......

In addition to the published articles, I have also contributed regular book reviews for our professional AEP Journal. The book reviews appeared in the following issues of the Journal.

AEP Journal Vol. 4, No.6
AEP Journal Vol. 5, No.1
AEP Journal Vol. 5, No.5
AEP Journal Vol. 5, No.10
AEP Journal Vol. 6, No.3

Educational Psychology in Practice Vol. 1, No.1
Educational Psychology in Practice Vol. 1, No.4 (Jan 1986)
Educational Psychology in Practice Vol. 4, No.2 (July 1988)
Educational Psychology in Practice Vol. 5, No.1 (April 1989)
Educational Psychology in Practice Vol. 6, No.1 (April 1990)
Educational Psychology in Practice Vol. 6, No.2 (July 1990)
Educational Psychology in Practice Vol. 6, No.3 (Oct 1990)
Educational Psychology in Practice Vol. 7, No.2 (July 1991)
Educational Psychology in Practice Vol. 8, No.4 (Jan 1993)

18549903R00095

Printed in Poland
by Amazon Fulfillment
Poland Sp. z o.o., Wrocław